My Forever
Memories,
Are Precious

My Forever Memories, Are Precious

Jo Ann D. Broome

Order this book online at www.trafford.com
or email orders@trafford.com

Most Trafford titles are also available at major online book retailers.

Printed in the United States of America.

ISBN: 978-1-4669-0117-9 (sc)
ISBN: 978-1-4669-0118-6 (e)

Library of Congress Control Number: 2011919115

Trafford rev. 11/08/2011

 www.trafford.com

North America & international
toll-free: 1 888 232 4444 (USA & Canada)
phone: 250 383 6864 ♦ fax: 812 355 4082

*This book is dedicated with love and honor to the Ones
responsible for bringing me into this world,
God,
and my Parents, Lester and Jessie Doub*

Chapter I

I T HAS ALWAYS been puzzling to me that my memory does not begin until I was five years old. At least, this was the first actual recollections I have of my life's beginning. There are many occasions that come to mind; however, I truly believe they are written on my mind's eye because I have heard them related many times by family, neighbors and friends. You know, you hear people say, "I will never forget the time you did this, or said this . . ." Then the story is related by someone and you are clueless as to what they are saying about you, or the incident they are describing. You don't remember it at all. I call these, "memory transfers."

The very first vivid memory for me occurred in the summer of 1943 when I was five years old. It was, for me, a time of excitement because I was going to be entering the first grade in school. In the 1940's I do not recall any of my friends who went to kindergarten. Maybe kindergarten was for the more affluent children at that time.

I had two brothers who were already in school, and I could not wait to be a part of the "*big school.*" No more '*play-likes*'—this was going to be *real* school.

My days of anticipation at entering school were filled with shopping for new school clothes, shoes, coats, everything I would be needing for my new adventure. At five years old, you don't have a concept of much that goes on with family and your life. Your needs are met by someone else—and your decisions are made for you as well. Life as I knew it was either a good or bad day. Happy or sad. Beyond that realm of thinking, it was not my responsibility. Little did I know that soon the excitement around my house would begin to turn to sadness.

Both of my parents were born in Winston—Salem, NC. When I came along my maternal and paternal grandparents were already deceased. Most of my aunts, uncles and cousins still lived in the North Carolina area. So my family, as I knew it, consisted of my Dad, Lester, my Mother Jessie, and two older brothers. Robert was 14 years old and mature far beyond his years. David was 12 years old and a real industrious boy for his age. He was always working at something to earn money. And then there was my dog Frisky, who was by no means a pedigree, but he was my best pal. We also had a cat named Kitty who was pretty much a community cat . . . she belonged to the last person who fed her.

Although my parents loved animals, Mom never allowed them to come inside the house. Dad had built a doghouse for Frisky beside our back screened in porch, but on stormy nights he would lay behind the shrubs outside my bedroom window and whine. I would have a hard time going to sleep just knowing Frisky was out in the storm. At the time, I thought my Mother was the most cruel person in the world. But Frisky survived. After all, David had found him abandoned in the woods. He had never had the luxury of being a house dog.

I was watching a TV program one evening where the host was asking a room full of kids to describe what their parents did for a living. Some of their answers were hilarious. And some did not have a clue what their parents did at their job. The kids were all between the ages of 4-6 years old. Somehow it made me think back to my concept of what my parents did when I was that age. Mother's job was easy. All she did was cook, clean house, wash clothes and iron, and take care of me. I knew that my Dad worked at a shop and fixed wrecked cars. I also knew that my Dad was the best Dad in the whole wide world. My brothers were always saying that I was 'daddy's little girl'.

My Mother and Daddy were the kind of parents that played with their children. They took us to church, to ballgames, on bicycle rides, walks around the neighborhood, and frequent picnics and the movies. We lived in a neighborhood that had children of all ages who played together, went to school and church together, and spent every waking hour just having fun. But, I was too young to know that there was a war going on in the world . . . that Uncle Sam had sent my Dad a letter of "Greetings" to come help fight this war. Nor did I realize that this auto body shop where my Dad worked was actually his business, the one that he had invested every penny of his savings into to establish himself in this work so he could provide for his family.

Daddy was very devoted to his family, and a good provider. Mother did not work outside the home. This was something that was just a given that she was the Mother of three children and she would stay home to take care of us and my Dad. It was important to my Daddy that we were provided the necessities of life. We certainly weren't rich, but there was enough love in our house to cover any lack of luxuries or wants we may have had. As most families in this generation, my Dad did not believe in credit. We waited until he had the money before we bought any extras such as furniture, cars, or anything other than the necessities. We always had a nice comfortable house, nice clean clothes, and sufficient food to eat. My Mom was such a thrifty person, she could take the least amount of anything and make it into the most delicious meal.

At any rate, my life at the age of five was the beginning of my life's experiences and memories. In the summer of 1943, as we were getting me prepared for entering school, I began to see my

Mom crying. She began to turn her attention even more towards my Dad and they spent a lot of time just sitting, talking. Because my Mother was always the most optimistic person I knew, always happy and busy taking care of her family, the sudden tears became something that I had never seen in her before. It also seemed that I was spending more time with my two brothers, and our next-door neighbors who had three older girls that treated me like their little sister.

Mother always wore an apron when she was in the kitchen, and that was a great deal of the time. This was before the frozen dinner meals and fast-food restaurants became popular. It seemed she was already preparing lunch as she was cleaning up the kitchen from breakfast. (No dishwasher either). And, early in the afternoon she began cooking for our supper meal. We didn't have a large refrigerator with a freezer to keep meats in, so Mother made almost daily trips to the local grocery to buy fresh vegetables and meats for meals. I grew up thinking that everyone ate three meals a day and on the schedule of 6:30 a.m. breakfast, noon lunch and 5:30-6:00 supper in the evening. For sure, meals around the table at our house were very special family times for us, and we kids were expected to be home at these times.

In the big pocket of this apron Mom wore, she always kept a nice clean handkerchief. I would notice her using this handkerchief more often, wiping tears from her eyes. Sometime when she was in the kitchen cooking, or while she was cleaning the house, she would just stop long enough to wipe her eyes. But we never talked about it. No one was telling me what was about to take place in my life. Around the last of August, and getting close to the time I was to begin school, my Dad seemed to be very busy preparing for something special. He was talking about duties my two brothers were to be responsible for. How they were to help out around the house. I wasn't involved with these conversations much because, as I look back now, I see that I was pretty well protected by my parents and my older brothers from the reality of what was about to take place in our family. My only concern at the time was my entry into the world of *'big school'*.

Up to this point in my life, my days were spent with my Mother. She was very active in our church and was always spending time helping out with various projects involving the church family and community. One of the sweet memories I have of a project that she always took care of each month was our visit to the "Old Folks Home." In those days it was quite different from our beautiful residential care and nursing home facilities we have now. I remember this particular home was located back in the woods at the end of a long dirt road. There were little wooden unpainted cottages that today would have been considered unlivable. They had no central heat and air-conditioning. In the winter the residents would sit around a wood-burning stove located in the middle of the room, wrapped up in coats and sweaters, and small blankets to keep warm. These garments were usually provided by various church ladies circles. In the summer they would sit outside under the large oak and elm trees for shade. The men would sit in their wooden slat chairs leaning against the big tree trunks. Everyone had a local funeral home paper fan that was moving as fast as they could to keep cool.

The fun part for me was that Mother let me distribute the hymn books, although I later learned that most of the residents there could neither read nor write. Some of them would not even know they had their hymnbooks turned upside down. But they could sing every word of every hymn or gospel song we would sing. Some of them could not see because they needed glasses . . . some could not eat anything very hard because they did not have proper teeth. Mother, and some of her friends from church, would always take refreshments. Kool Aid and cookies were the usual refreshment in the summer time. And cookies and hot chocolate were their favorite in the winter. On some visits we took them little sandwiches which they loved.

The program consisted of visiting with each person, someone would read Scripture from the Bible and give a short devotion and then we would sing. These folks were big on Amens and Hallelujahs. They didn't say these much in my church so this was nice. I learned that these expressions meant that they *really* approved of what you were saying. After the prayer time, Mother would always let me pass out the napkins, cookies and Kool Aid. I must have been in my teen years before I realized that every black lady was not named Annie! It seemed my Mother told me to call most of the ladies "Miss Annie." Years later I found out that this place was actually called the "Alms House." It was a facility provided by the county where they sent people who were virtually homeless and without any relatives to take care of them. They had no Medicare or Medicaid to help take care of them back then. They were truly wards of the State and County. The only thing that I recall about this event that I did not enjoy, was the fact that they always seemed to have a 'funny odor' about them. It was also much later when I learned that some of the cabins did not have running water.

To this day, I can actually say that this trip to the nursing home each month had a lasting affect on me, because I have always had a special place in my heart for individuals who are placed in facilities by family, or States, and are virtually forgotten as human beings. I still visit assisted living facilities, give out hymn books, lead the singing, pray and serve refreshments. It is quite different now. The places I go have central heat, air-conditioning, beautiful furnishings and decorations, fresh flowers all around and serve delicious food. I'm sure that the residents at the facilities I go to now would not be as proud of a cup of Kool Aid and a little cookie as these folks were. I thank God for the progress we've made in this area of caring for our elderly and physically impaired.

CHAPTER 2

WE HAD THE best neighbors next door named the Byrds. There was Uncle Roscoe, a short stocky built man with a beautiful head of curly hair. He was such a hard worker. Always had a bountiful vegetable garden each year with the best watermelons and tomatoes, which he generously shared with the neighbors. Aunt Lula Mae was a very attractive, articulate lady. She had long hair that she pulled up into a bun and always wore the prettiest house dresses. Ladies in this generation did not wear long pants, and even if they did, they would never be caught out in public with anything other than a dress or suit on. Even when Aunt Lula Mae would help Uncle Roscoe work in the garden, she would always have on a pretty dress. I called them Aunt and Uncle because my parents would not allow us to call them by their first names. As it turned out in my life, they were more my grandparents than neighbors.

There were three Byrd girls. Vera, the oldest, Doris (Tootsie), the middle girl, and Sybil the youngest. My two brothers were ages that were in between the oldest and youngest of the Byrd girls. We were not just neighbors, we were like family. We went to church together, they attended school with my brothers. I became their 'little sister' and was treated very special. I knew they loved me by the way they took care of me. "Tootsie" took me everywhere with her. We went to movies, shopping, ballgames and church. She let me dress up in her big clothes and shoes . . . even used makeup. She always had such pretty things. I had long hair and Tootsie always loved to brush it for me. Aunt Lula Mae made many of the clothes her girls wore. One particular coat I remember, was the coat she made for me that matched her girls' coats. It was navy blue with a big white collar. There was no question that I felt like family when they made a picture with their pretty new coats, and I was standing in front-looking just like one of them.

One of the fondest memories I have of Aunt Lula Mae, as I was allowed to refer to her with much affection, was her beautiful yard. She had the most gorgeous flowers that were set in areas where she had swings and benches covered with roses winding around trellises. Some of the flowers created such a sweet fragrance that you thought you were in a perfume store. I would sneak across the street to be with her while she was working in her flowers. She would stop her work, fix us a snack and a drink and we would sit in the swing for long periods, just talking about her flowers, about God's creation and how He made everything so beautiful and for a purpose.

It was on one of the days Aunt Lula Mae and I were having our little tea party and chat, when she somehow had sensed that I was saddened about my Mother's crying. She told me what was going on in my family that was causing my Mom to be sad and cry. She opened the conversation by asking if I would like to spend several nights with her girls while my Mother went to Mississippi with my Dad. They would be leaving in a few days and would be riding on the train. Mom would be coming home, without my Dad for a while, but he was going to be okay and that I would be very proud of him for what he was going to do.

Now, this seemed to be more than I could understand at the time, because there were so many questions I asked Aunt Lula Mae. She must have told my parents they would have to try to explain. Questions like.—"Why I must stay with her family? Why my Mom and Dad were leaving together and why my Mom would be coming home without Dad for a while?" A child of five does not have the reasoning ability to understand the true meaning of what a war is, or why you have to be separated from your loving parents, and why you have to leave your home and spend time with neighbors. So, the time had come when the reality of all the sadness and tears, the very busy days and urgent plans were to unfold for me. Although I didn't fully understand, I knew that things around my house, and in my family were changing.

I remember the afternoon my Dad took me on one of our many afternoon walks around the neighborhood, holding hands, talking and laughing, acting silly. Always recalling the love that flowed from him to me through those hands that seemingly always had a little paint on them and smelled of paint thinner and Lava soap. As we walked, he began to tell me what he was going to have to do, how long he planned to be away from me and how I was to be the smartest girl in Watkins School. I was to say my prayers, help my Mother when she needed me, and remember always how much he loved me. Truthfully this was the very first memory I have of being *sad*. It was not a story that had been told to me that I had heard repeated, but it was an emotion etched in my memory *forever*. It touched my heart and saddened me that my Daddy was going away.

Memories can be good ones, or they can be bad. They can be happy ones, or they can be sad. Some of our memories are created from small events that happen which seem to be so insignificant. And then there are special occasions in our lives that create memories that are *forever* etched in our minds. In my life, there are a few memories that I would like to have deleted because of the hurt they still bring to mind. For me, some of the most precious memories are the little insignificant ones.

Like the incident told by Aunt Lula Mae and her daughters of the time when I was around three years old. It seems it was an almost daily ritual that Mom and Aunt Lula Mae would sit on the porch, drink coffee and discuss various things, and I'm sure plan their day ahead. One particular day, while they were sitting on the porch in deep conversation, I was busy visiting Aunt Lula Mae's flower gardens next door. I was not just *visiting* the gardens, I was actually *picking* Aunt Lula Mae's beautiful tulips. Not by the long stems at the bottom, but by the short tulip tops. When I came across the street and approached the porch where Mom and Aunt Lula Mae were sitting, I was carrying the most beautiful bouquet of tulips you've ever seen. None of them long enough to put in a vase of water. I had picked every one of the tulips blooming at the time in her lovely flower gardens. The story goes of how I was scolded for this little escapade by my Mother, but Aunt Lula Mae's girls were furious. The reason they were so angry was because they had all wanted to pick a bouquet to carry to their teachers and Aunt Lula Mae refused to let them pick a one. The other reason the girls were so angry was that *their* mother would not let *my* Mother punish me for picking the flowers. I am in my seventies now and to this day, they have never let me live this little *'flower picking'* trip down. It has been told again and again, and each time embellished quite a bit I'm sure. This was truly one of the "transferred memories" I have because I do not remember this at all. It may very well be one reason that to this day, I am reluctant to cut many of my flowers from my flower garden. I love to see them bloom outdoors where everyone can enjoy them. Many flower gardeners have different feelings about cutting their flowers. Some hold to the belief that the more you cut, the more flowers you produce. Quite frankly, I have no recollection of this incident, but it is one I will always be reminded of by the Byrd girls.

Well, the day finally arrived in late August, when my Mother and Dad boarded the train for Mississippi. I did not go to the train station. I was being entertained by the Byrd girls next door. They felt that my seeing my Mom and Dad get on the train would be too traumatic for me. Up to this point in my life, I had never been away from my parents. This was the beginning of a three day stay with my neighbors. My brothers were old enough to stay across the street at our house and take care of themselves. They were both very responsible and could carry out all the chores they were to look after. Uncle Roscoe took them under his wing and saw that they had all they needed to take care of their responsibilities at the house. In the evening they would eat at the Byrd's house and then stay in our house at night. In those days, there was little fear that they could not handle the duties they had been assigned by our Dad before he left. Nor was there any concern that they would be in any danger by themselves.

During the days spent with Aunt Lula Mae and Uncle Roscoe, and the girls, I was kept occupied and distracted from what was happening in my family. They talked about school, we continued to shop for clothes and school supplies. One of my favorite things was my pencil box. It was bright red. It was a heavy duty cardboard box that had a drawer that pulled out in front. It contained pencils, crayons, a pencil sharpener, an eraser, some paper scissors and a ruler. Everything I'd need to begin my education. I remember taking the things out of this pencil box several times a day, reorganizing them with such anticipation at being able to actually use them in '*big school*'. My brothers would say, "Sis, you're going to wear those things out before you start school." But is was mine and I was so proud of it. I also had a little book bag. Nothing like the backpacks that the kids now have, but it had a flap that buckled over it with a handle . . . I was feeling pretty big about this time in my life. And, even though the world around me was changing in ways that would eventually affect me for the rest of my life, this moment was the *best* time of my life, or at least I remember it being so.

Isn't it wonderful that when you are surrounded by people who love you, that nothing in the world seems to be too big to handle? Although my Mom and Dad had gone away and I had learned that my Dad would not be coming home with her, I was still content with my situation, because of my wonderful neighbors caring for me. They always made me feel loved. Nighttime was the time I missed my Mom and Dad the most.

Uncle Roscoe used to make 'hoe-cake'. It was made like a large fat pancake in an iron skillet, but is was so fluffy. The way he taught me to eat it was to break it off in small pieces and 'sop' it around in my plate of sorghum syrup and fresh butter. This was a treat that I will never forget. I remember that sometimes after we had our evening meal, Uncle Roscoe would get out the big iron skillet and syrup . . . I knew what was coming. It was the best dessert I ever had. At least I thought it was dessert.

Finally the day came for my Mother to come home on the train. Aunt Lula Mae dressed me in one of my new school dresses and we went down to the train station on Gervais Street in Columbia to meet her. That was the first time I had been that close to a real passenger train and I remember they had benches along the tracks where we waited. It was late in the evening and when I saw the big lights of the engine and heard the loud whistle blow, I can still remember my stomach feeling like it was going to turn upside-down. I began to cry, not from sadness, but from the excitement of having my Mom come home. When the train finally slowed down and pulled along side the station, I could see the people sitting by the windows. Some of them waving to relatives and friends. And then I saw her. She was the most beautiful lady I had ever seen. She was tall, had the brightest, clear blue eyes that seemed to smile all the time. Mother always wore a hat and gloves when she got all dressed up to go somewhere. She was a very elegant lady and I was so happy when she stepped off the train. But, there was already something missing—my Dad was not standing beside her.

As we rode home, Mom was telling us all about her trip, how Daddy looked so handsome in his Navy uniform and how he sent his love to us all. Even before we arrived home, I remember feeling sad that my Dad would not be there to tuck me in. To kiss me goodnight and say, 'sleep tight, and don't let the bedbugs bite'. This was our sign-off every night until I left home. I never out-grew it. I have a little needlepoint pillow on my guest bed with this saying on it. And I never walk into that room and see it that I don't have memories of my Dad.

Things at home didn't seem to change that much, for a while at least. My brothers followed my Dad's instructions about chores, I helped my Mom, as much as she would let me, and my neighbors seemed to always be there for us, to help in any way they could. School started and I was so excited to be able to finally get to wear all my new school clothes and shoes. And of course, to be able to carry my new book bag with my new pencil box inside . . . I was *ready* for the big day.

I remember meeting my first grade teacher, Miss Dunlap. She was tall and slender, like my Mom, and she had a sweet smile, just like my Mom. I knew that this was the best thing that had ever happened to me. I remember it so well. This was a memory I made for my very own 'memory book'. When you can close your eyes and recall vividly a place or a situation, these are memories no one can erase or change in your mind.

As I walked into that classroom on my first day at school, it was all decorated with big letters of the alphabet and numbers. There were beautiful pictures and posters all around the room, and bookshelves with so many little books in them. And she had pretty flower pots sitting all around the room, just like my Mom had at home. There were boys and girls, some I already knew from my neighborhood and church friends. And then there were some that would become my 'new friends' who would continue with me through the next twelve years in school. It was my first impression of what '*big school*' was all about and, as they say, first impressions are usually the most important ones we will have in an experience.

CHAPTER 3

As the year went by, I began to see some changes taking place in our family. One was that we were packing up to move to another house. It wasn't very far from where we lived and I would still be in the same school. I don't remember asking why we were moving, but as Mother was always the optimistic one, she assured me that it was for the best. Now I was six years old, having celebrated my sixth birthday in November after school began. Robert was now 15 and David was 13. Robert always seemed to be big for his age. He was tall, blonde and very handsome. He seemed to be taking the initiative of my Dad when it came to making some of the decisions that our family made. Robert was already driving. We had an older 1937 Chevrolet that had running boards on it. I remember that the house where we moved to had a driveway that was a little below the roadway into the yard. Robert would leave the car at the top of the drive so it could roll down to start up the next morning.

Our new house, not new, but *new* to us, had three bedrooms, a large living room with a fireplace, a dining room, and a kitchen that had a Warm Morning two burner coal burning stove that we had to dress by in the morning to keep from freezing. There was a large heater room that all of the other rooms opened to, including the one bathroom which was the coldest place in the house. We didn't use this stove all the time because of the cost of fuel oil. Mom would turn the big heater off at night when we went to bed. We used the fireplace in the living room and the Warm Morning stove in the kitchen for heat. By the time the house got warm during the day, it was time to go to bed and Mom would turn the heat off again. I remember very well trying to sit on the toilet seat that I was sure had been kept in the refrigerator all night.

It was not until much later that I learned the real reason we moved into our new house. It was larger, and my Mother had figured out that she could rent out one of the bedrooms to an army wife whose husband was stationed at Fort Jackson, and this would help with our expenses. So, I moved in with Mom, my brothers had one bedroom and the wife of the soldier rented the extra bedroom. She helped Mom with the housework, cooking and other chores as well. She was a lot of fun and it appeared that our family was again back to normal, at least as normal as we could be considering the circumstances.

Both of my brothers had paper routes. Robert would get up at 4:30 in the mornings and deliver papers to Fort Jackson

Army Base. David would go with him and then they would come home and get ready for school. It was obvious that Robert was becoming 'my dad' during these times. He was helpful to Mom and did his part in every way to keep our family comfortable and happy. He would go down to Dad's auto shop after school each day and work until time to come home in the evening.

David was very industrious as well. He added another job of delivering groceries after school on his bicycle for friends of our family who owned the local neighborhood grocery store. He also had his afternoon paper route delivering the Columbia Record. He taught me how to fold the papers so he could throw them onto the neighbors porches without having to get off his bike. They had to be folded so they looked almost like a postage stamp.

I don't know how my family would have survived without the help of my two brothers. Looking back over this time in our family life makes me so proud of my two brothers. I don't remember their ever complaining. It seemed we always had something to be happy about. That's such a treasured memory for me.

I guess I was the only one that was "unemployed" . . . The only jobs I had were helping Mom, drying dishes and setting the table for meals. I didn't get paid for these jobs. My memory at this time was of playing with the two grandchildren of a black family who lived in a house that sat in a field behind our house. They were our closest neighbors at the time, and the only children I had to play with close by. There was a boy named Willie, and a girl named Sarah. I was fascinated with Sarah because she had her hair platted in little pigtails with ribbons on each one. I had long hair and Mother platted my hair in pigtails, but I only had two long pigtails. I remember wanting more with the ribbons on them like Sarah's. Sarah, Willie and I used to have tea parties on our front porch, which consisted of Kool Aid and cookies. In those days, we could not go into each others houses to visit, so Sarah and I would swap dolls. She would take mine home to spend the night and I would keep hers. Sarah liked my dolls because they had extra clothes you could change, and I liked her dolls because they were made of soft socks that had faces sewn on them. They had no clothes at all. I'm sure her grandmother made them for her but they were always so soft and cuddly, and I remember the nights I held them by my pillow as I slept. Now the thing I remember about little Willie was his hair. His hair stood up high on his head and looked almost like my mother's Brillo pads. I always wanted to just feel it, but I never did. We were good friends, but when we moved away I never saw them again.

We had other neighbors who lived down the road from us. They lived in a big white house that, compared to our house, was a mansion. They each drove a big fancy car. They didn't have any children, and the thing I do remember about this family was that they would never stop to pick us up when we were walking to school, even on rainy cold days. They would just drive right on by us. The roads we traveled getting to school were not paved and in rainy weather they were pretty muddy. Guess they just didn't want us to *muddy up* their fancy cars.

On some really cold mornings our old '37 Chevy would not crank up so my brothers would go out to the end of the road and hitch-hike a ride with someone to get to school. My Mom would bundle the two of us up and begin our walk to my school, which was exactly one mile from our house. Then she would walk the mile back home. The road was not paved and it only had about three houses along the way between our house and the school. The rest of the area was wooded. If the car warmed up enough to start during the day, Mom drove to pick me up. If not, I would come to the gate on the side of the school yard and there she would be waiting for me outside, all wrapped up and sometimes with an umbrella if it was raining. She would have a thermos with hot chocolate in it to warm me on our walk back home. Later I came to realize just why my Mother was so slim and healthy. She was one of the hardest workers and walked so much. I never recall a day that she was sick enough to stay in bed. I'm sure there were days when she didn't feel like getting up, but she did. I grew up thinking that we weren't allowed to 'get sick'. Mom believed in a big dose of Phillips Milk of Magnesia at least once a month. At least it didn't taste as bad as Castor Oil. In the winter she would rub my chest with Vicks. These home remedies worked great because I never remember having to see a doctor.

One scary memory I have of the walk between school and our house, was the day when I came out to go home. Mother was not there waiting for me. After waiting for her for some time, I started walking home—, alone. As I approached a certain place in the road, there were high banks on either side of the road and I saw military tanks, jeeps and soldiers all over the hillsides with rifles. It was a very frightening sight for me, but I continued to walk on. Still no sight of my Mother. I looked up to see this soldier coming towards me with his rifle on his shoulder . . . As he approached me, he told me not to be afraid that they were military on maneuvers and they would not harm me. He asked me where I lived. I told him and that my Mother would be coming to meet me. But as we were talking, two other soldiers came up and the three of them escorted me on down the road towards my house until I saw my Mother come running to meet us. I will never forget the beautiful sight of my Mother as she approached me. Of course she knew what the soldiers were doing in the area, and she knew that they would in no way harm me, but as I looked at her she began to cry. I think it was because she was so sorry that something had kept her from being at the school to pick me up. That experience was certainly one of the first ones that taught me that I could walk the distance from school by myself, and it must have given me great courage at the time. I always wanted to do things on my own, just like my two older brothers.

Our neighborhood at the time was sparsely developed. There was a family named Dents that lived above us. They had a son named Billy who was more the age of my brothers. They had quite a lot of land and ran a dairy for a while. I remember the large barns and the animals they owned. Even though they lived just across the road, the house and barn sat quite a distance from our house. We could not see lights from any of our neighbors, and we didn't have any street lights. On moonless nights, IT WAS DARK! We were never brought up to be afraid. Even as a child I was never afraid. I don't remember ever having a key to our house. It wasn't necessary because we didn't lock our doors when we left. I was born in 1938 and lived at home with my parents until 1960 when I married. I *never* owned a house key. Our cars sat in the back yard, no carport or garage, and the keys were either left in the ignition or in the floorboard of the front seat of each car. Now we don't even feel safe in our homes with door locks, deadbolts and our cars in enclosed garages.

Chapter 4

I T WAS NOT easy to get everything we needed during the war. I remember helping David collect and flatten tin cans with a hammer. We would load up his wagon and haul them about a quarter mile to a man who delivered them to the scrap dealer to process for materials used in the war. I also remember saving my dimes to buy savings stamps at school. We put them in a little booklet and this was our way of helping our government pay for the war . . . the one that had taken my Dad off on a ship somewhere in the Pacific Ocean.

During the time that Dad was away, we made many adjustments in our living habits. There was no doubt that Uncle Sam wasn't providing a life of luxury for the families of servicemen. We had ration stamps for food, gasoline, fuel oil and other necessities. Our friends who owned the local community grocery store provided extra items such as cans of salmon when they had them. I remember salmon particularly because Mom used to have them with eggs and grits for breakfast, and one of my favorite meals was her salmon patties in the evening with grits. I think I was grown when I finally found out that *grits* was not a required 'vegetable' with each meal.

We took walks through the woods with David's wagon to pick up wood for the fireplace, and in the evenings when it was time to go to bed, Mother would take a towel and wrap around a glass quart jar filled with steaming hot water to put between the sheets so my feet would not be cold. In the morning I would wake up and find the bottle as cold as the toilet seat.

As the saying goes, 'you never miss things you've never had'. These war-time days were so different for our family with Daddy away. Now in hindsight, I realize that we were far from being rich, at least in the sense of monetary terms, but we had food to eat, clean clothes and enough love in our family with friends to carry us through several wars. Our church family was our extended family. We had always been taught that our religious worship and commitment to service was part of our daily lives. Since I did not have living grandparents, I grew up feeling that everyone in my church was my grandmother or grandfather. I loved going to church. I was not only 'Daddy's baby', I was Crescent Hill Baptist Church's baby. Mom took me to church on Sundays when I was only two weeks old. She sat on the back pew and laid me on a bed pillow.

Mother would receive a letter occasionally from my Dad. Usually she would read it to me because Daddy would always say in it, tell Jo to "sleep tight and don't let the bedbugs bite." There would be some things Mom would not read aloud to me, and I could see the worry in her eyes as she would take the handkerchief from her apron pocket to wipe a tear from her eyes as she continued reading some of those letters. One letter I remember was sad for me. It included a picture of my Dad sitting in a wheelchair in front of a Christmas tree. He was opening a gift and some other sailors were all standing around him and the tree. I could not understand why he was sitting in a wheelchair and I questioned Mother about this. I always related people sitting in wheelchairs as being crippled or sick. Her answer was that he had been a little sick, but he was going to be alright.

Our Christmas traditions have always been kept in a special place in my 'Memory Book'. Like most families, we had our own traditions. One week before Christmas we would go into the woods, find a small cedar tree and cut it down. Daddy would make a wooden stand for it and mom would put a little pan of water under the tree trunk to keep the tree fresh. On the evening we decorated the tree, Dad would bring home fresh oysters for a stew for supper. After supper we would get the box of decorations down from the attic. Every tree decoration we owned was stored in one cardboard box. We used the same lights and decorations year after year. Mother would turn on the radio so we could listen to Christmas Carols and sing-a-long. It was Dad's job to check out the tree lights and put them on the tree. Sometimes he would spend hours working on the two strings of colored glass lights. Sometimes re-wiring the whole string, or replacing the bulbs or the plug. Each string of lights only had eight light bulbs on it, so it didn't take long to put lights on the tree. My brothers and I would put on the decorations we had and hang the *new* silver tinsel. After the tree was all decorated, Mom would pop corn and fix hot chocolate. We would cut out the lights, sit by our open fireplace, listen to the Christmas music and enjoy our beautiful Christmas tree. Looking back on these days, I always remember our little cedar tree being the most beautiful Christmas tree in the world to me. Compared to all the fancy trees and decorations we now are able to buy, our Christmas tree must have rated up there pretty close to a "Charlie Brown Christmas Tree."

When I think of all the strings of 100 light bulbs that I have thrown in the trash in recent years, sometimes simply because I couldn't get them untangled, and the Christmas ornaments, garlands and, even some artificial trees that have been hauled to the trash dump . . . it reminds me of just how *precious* each string of lights, and each ornament was to us back in those days. It also makes me feel a bit ashamed that I have lost my value of these family traditions. When I was a child, Christmas was celebrated for its 'True Meaning'.

I never remember a large number of Christmas presents under our tree, even on Christmas after Santa came on his visits. But—I also never remember not being happy with what I did receive on Christmas. I guess the only sadness I remember was the first Christmas my Dad was away in service. It was the first one being spent in our present house and Mother had already sat us down and told us that we would not be able to enjoy a big Christmas that year because of Daddy's being away and things being pretty tight. But this did not keep us from carrying out our Christmas traditions when it came to having a Christmas tree. We cut down a small cedar tree and decorated it with our usual decorations. We made paper chains, had candy canes and used the same lights we'd used years before. That year the lights for the tree didn't need any repair.

Entertainment was not very eventful at this time in our lives, but one of my favorite things to do with my Mom was to go downtown Columbia and window shop. (I know why we spent so much time doing this . . . it didn't cost any money to look!) We would ramble through the dime stores. One in particular was Silver's Dime Store on Main Street. It had everything you could ever want in it, from live goldfish in a tank to little turtles with painted scenes on their backs. They sold groceries in the back of the store and had a lunch counter with stools where you could sit and eat. They sold clothing, shoes, linens. It was the 'cheap' version of a general store or department store. They even had a music section. It was no bigger than a closet, but it had a piano and racks of popular sheet music. The lady who played the piano was a short, chubby, white-haired lady who could really tickle the keys of the old upright piano. I would go stand in front of the music racks and pull a piece of sheet music and she would play it for me. Mother would do her shopping and come back to get me . . . I was still standing right where she left me . . . just listening to the music being played on the old piano.

Mother would let me look through all the aisles at the many trinkets, and for weeks I had focused my eyes on a little cedar chest on one of the counters. It had a beautiful scene painted on the top, and the fascination of the box was that it had this tiny key so you could lock it up. Now, I can't imagine why a six year old would need a key to her cedar chest, but it was one of the fascinations of the little chest. Perhaps it was because my two brothers both had Tampa Nugget cigar boxes in their dresser drawers that had written all over them, "Private Property, Keep Out, None of Your Business." I guess I thought I could lock my personal things up in *my* little 'private box'. Every time Mother and I would go to town, we would end up in Silver's Dime Store looking at the little cedar chest. That was all I wanted, but I knew what Mom had already told us about not expecting Santa to bring us anything for Christmas.

On the night before Christmas, one of our traditions was to sit by the fireplace, drink hot chocolate and sing Christmas Carols. We would sometimes enjoy our popcorn again and just have a truly wonderful time together as Dad would read the Christmas story from the Bible. Well, Christmas Eve wasn't the most joyful time for us that year, but we made the best of it. There were a few pretty ragged looking packages under the tree, but it certainly lacked our usual display of gifts at Christmas. One of the packages contained a box of handkerchiefs that I had bought for Mom from Silver's Dime Store with twenty-five cents that my brother Robert had given to me to shop for Mom's present.

The next morning Mother got up early to build the fire in the fireplace, turned on the Christmas tree lights and had breakfast cooking. That year it seemed we knew we didn't have to get up so early because there weren't many presents under the tree and Mom had already prepared us for a slim Christmas. We went in and sat warming ourselves by the fireplace and Mother began handing out some little packages. Some of them had not been under the tree when we went to bed the night before so I was sure that Santa had made a stop at our house during the night. Every one received one gift. They weren't much, but they were items we all needed. Mostly clothes and socks. Of course when my Mother opened her gift from me, you would have thought it was the finest mink coat she had every seen. It was the little box of embroidered handkerchiefs I had bought for twenty-five cents in Silver's Dime Store.

I did not see where Santa had made a visit to our house to leave anything like a baby doll or anything that he usually brought. But, Robert said, "Sis, why don't you look in back of the tree, there is something back there." So I got down under the tree and pulled out this box. It had my name on it from SANTA. I opened the box and what do you think was inside? The little cedar chest with the beautiful painting on the top with the little gold key attached that I had been wishing for, and visiting for weeks before Christmas at Silver's Dime Store. I could not believe it. Now I truly did believe there was a real Santa.

It was not until I was older that I learned how my two brothers, Robert and David, had been working at their paper routes, and delivering groceries to earn enough extra money to buy me this special gift. This little cedar chest stayed with me through my years growing up. I had it when I married in 1960 and finally passed it on to a niece of mine. It still had the beautiful painting on the top and the little gold key was still hanging behind it. Through the years it held so many memories. Not because of the value of it, but for the love and sacrifices made by my two brothers to make my Christmas wish come true.

Chapter 5

My first year of school had so many 'first experiences' for me. Learning to read and write, to have all those new friends to play with, and a teacher who truly showed her love for teaching you. It laid the foundation for my interest and love of school. When I look back over the years at age 5 and 6, it is so hard to believe that one little girl could have so many changes and experiences within a one year period. It makes it easier to make the statement that, for me, my first real memories began at the age of five.

While my Dad was away, even though I still could not understand what a war was, I did realize that it was something scary, because there were times at night when we would have to sit in the dark and we could hear airplanes flying overhead. I think is was what they called "black-outs." Well, it seemed so long since I had seen my Daddy . . . I missed him, his laughter, his teasing me and especially our walks in the neighborhood. Of course it would all be new to him when he came home this time, because we had moved while he was gone. Or at least I thought that we would be in the same house. But, as I was beginning to learn, things in life change quickly because one evening after our supper, Mother sat us around the kitchen table, that was where we gathered for meals and talks about important things as a family. Mom told us that the people who were renting our previous house were moving out and we would be moving back to our house next door to the Byrd family. Now I could not have been happier because I had truly missed being with this family and having the three girls spending time with me and taking me places. So, we packed up our belongings and someone loaned us a pick-up truck. My brothers were getting pretty big now and our former neighbors were right there to help us move back into the neighborhood. It took us three days to move everything. Even though we did not have a lot of furniture. We had three bedroom suites, living and dining room furniture and tables and chairs, and of course our clothes.

Shortly after we moved back to our house next door to the Byrd family, Robert and David had the idea that since times were pretty tough and meat wasn't that plentiful, they could help out. They built a pig pen and we bought two little pigs. The plan was to fatten the pigs, and slaughter them for meat. Well, as you would imagine, pigs are cute when they're little. They had names and quickly became part of our family. When the time came for slaughtering, my brothers could not kill them. Uncle Roscoe had to load them up and take them to a meatpacking house to have them processed. I can recall the tears shed when Uncle Roscoe drove out of the yard with those two pigs in his truck. I don't remember if we ever ate any of the meat after it was processed. Somehow it never seemed right that we were eating two of our family pets.

I do know that was the end of my brothers 'pig-farming' days. It also determined at an early age that neither Robert nor David would succeed in skills of architectural design or building contractors. Their pig pen was little more than a three sided shanty with sheets of tin for a roof. Pigs must be pretty dumb, because the only thing necessary for their freedom would have been for them to lean on the pen or fence and they would have been '*free little piggies.*'

DAD COMES HOME

Not long after we had moved and gotten settled in our house, Mother told us that Daddy was going to be coming home. But, he was going to have to spend some time in the hospital in Augusta, Georgia. Now that was upsetting for me, because being in a hospital meant that he was sick or injured. Actually, I'm not sure at the time that my Mother even realized the condition of my Dad, but she did know that he had experienced a complete nervous breakdown while he was in the Navy. The excitement I felt that Daddy was coming home was what gave me my ability to try to understand what my Mother was trying to explain to me. There were going to be some more changes in our lives when he got home.

Mother had made arrangements to be with him in Augusta for a while to help him recover from his condition before he came home to our family. She had rented a room at a boarding house across from the hospital in Augusta for a few weeks. And again, I was going to be staying with our neighbors next door during that time. They would see that I was taken care of. Nowhere could I go that I would have been happier, and loved more than with the Byrd family.

It was early spring of 1945 when my Dad finally arrived in Augusta. The hardest thing for me to understand was that I could not go visit him. Even at six years old, I knew something was wrong that they would not let me go to visit my Dad. I remember crying myself to sleep at night and how Aunt Lula Mae would hold me and talk to me. She would pray with me and ask God to take care of Mom and Dad. We'd pray for God to help him get well and come home soon. Uncle Roscoe would make his famous "hoe-cake" and we would sop our syrup and butter . . . but, none of this took away the loneliness that I felt at not being able to see my Daddy.

It was a beautiful spring because I remember the daffodils and tulips in Aunt Lula Mae's yard were blooming. One day after I had come home from school, Aunt Lula Mae took me outside and we sat in the swing for a long time. It always seemed she sensed exactly what was going on in my mind, and the sadness I was experiencing at this time in my life. And, it seemed, she always knew the perfect words to say to make me feel better.

She began to tell me some of the things that had happened to cause my Dad's illness. She said that my Dad was thirty-nine years old, with a wife and three children and only a few months earlier had invested his life savings to go into a business for himself. Dad had received the draft notice from Uncle Sam, and the time period he had before reporting for active duty, they gave him less than a month to close his business or find someone to run it for him while he was away. My Dad had made the choice of going into the Navy. She told me that many of his friends, them included, had tried to get him to apply for an exemption because of his situation and age, but Daddy would not even consider this. So Daddy had found someone he thought could take over and run the business for him until he got out of service. Someone he trusted with his life savings investment. It was believed that because of the stress and worry of being away from his wife and family, and concern about the business that he had just started up, the mental worry was too much for him. Daddy was always devoted to taking care of his family, and even in a wartime situation, he could not stop thinking of what was happening to his family and business back home. Mother told me in later years that the only time she deliberately lied to Daddy was in her letters to him while he was away in service. He was always asking how we were getting along and she told him we were doing just fine. She did not want him to worry that we were having it pretty hard with his being away.

All of the things Aunt Lula Mae was telling me were a bit difficult for me to understand. I just wanted to *see* my Daddy. I needed to see that he was alright. But this would not happen until later after I had gotten out of school for the summer. I vividly remember one Friday night before I went to bed, Aunt Lula Mae told me that Mother was coming home on Saturday and she was taking me to Augusta to see my Dad on Sunday. Aunt Lula Mae had gotten my prettiest dress and my black patent leather shoes ready for me to wear. I was so excited, but I also did not know what to expect. After all, Daddy had been at the hospital for several months now and there was no talk of his coming home. But on Saturday, mother came home and we made plans for she and I to drive down to Augusta on Sunday to visit Daddy. I remember sleeping with her on Saturday night . . . oh, it was so good to cuddle up with her and listen as she talked to me about Dad. I could hear the love in her voice, but I could also detect some sadness. She explained that when I saw him, he would be looking a bit thin and would be very nervous. I was not to startle him in any way and I would need to be as quiet as I could be.

On Sunday morning I was so excited that I was going to see my Dad. I got all dressed up in my Sunday School clothes. Mother had washed my hair and rolled it. I had real long curly hair that Daddy loved to brush for me. He would brush it for me after mother washed it, and he would be so gentle getting the tangles out of it. He didn't hurt nearly as much as Mom did. I remember that Aunt Lula Mae came over very early before she and her family went to church to bring us a picnic basket to take down to eat with my Dad on the hospital grounds. She had fried chicken, potato salad, pimento cheese sandwiches which were my favorite, and a big jug of lemonade. She had baked a chocolate layer cake. She knew this was Dad's favorite.

Our family was big on picnics. Mother seemed to always have the ingredients to pack up a picnic basket anytime someone suggested it. She was a great cook and always prepared meals for us that were healthy with vegetables and fruits. The Byrds had a beautiful garden each year and we always were the recipients of fresh produce. With everything that was taking place with my Dad in the hospital, Mother was showing signs of losing weight, and she was already a very slender lady. I'm sure the stress of my Dad's illness, and her having to be away from our family was beginning to put a strain on her physically, as well as mentally. But Mother never complained. She was the most energetic, optimistic person in my life, no matter what the circumstances were at the time.

When Mom and I arrived at the hospital in Augusta, it was a shock to see they had a guard on the entrance gates. I had visited hospitals with my parents as a child, but never had I seen a guard outside a fence before. The guard actually had a rifle by his side. As we entered the hospital, we could not go to Daddy's room. We had to wait in a specific waiting area and the nurses brought him to us. The anticipation was so great that I could actually feel my stomach feeling sick. This would be the first time I had seen my Dad since he left home in late summer of 1943.

As if this visit was actually taking place today, I can remember the first sight I had of my Dad. His beautiful loving eyes were set so far back in his head and he looked so pale and thin. The smile I remembered was gone from his face. I could tell that he was very nervous because he was actually shaking all over. He was dressed in his pajamas and housecoat. He stood there looking at me as if he was seeing me for the very first time. I wanted to run to his arms and hug him, but Mother held my hand and waited to see how he was going to respond. After a few minutes of our just staring at each other, I remember him opening his arms wide and I ran to him as fast as I could. I remember his holding me without saying one word, but running his hand through my long curls and touching my face. We were both crying, but I heard him say, "my beautiful little girl, I love you so." For that precious moment, it was the happiest day of my life to have my Daddy holding me again.

We took our picnic basket out onto the grounds under some tremendous trees and spread our blanket and tablecloth to enjoy our first meal together after he had returned from the war. I remember seeing men standing around the grounds. They were just standing still, like they were standing at attention as soldiers. Mother told me that some of these soldiers had come home "shell-shocked" from the war. They did not know where they were. The nurses brought them outside each day, weather permitting, and they stood there until someone came to get them. Oh, there were so many things that had changed since my Dad had left home . . . too many things that I could not understand.

At least my Dad didn't have to stand at attention all day. To this day, I can get very emotional at times when we celebrate the 4th of July, Memorial Day and Veterans' Day. The red, white and blue of our American Flag bring back memories of sacrifices made by our military, and how war can change our loved ones, *forever*.

After spending a few more months in Augusta, Mother told my brothers and me that Daddy would be coming home. We talked about how we were to be very quiet around the house. We could not drop anything that would make a loud, startling noise. I could not play the radio loud, and not at all after he had gone to bed at night. Because my bedroom was at the other end of the house from my parents bedroom, this was easier for me to do. I spent a lot of time next door at my neighbors while my Dad recuperated.

One day Dad and I went on one of our long walks around the neighborhood. We had only walked about a block from the house and I was lagging behind him. I ran up behind him and grabbed him around the waist. The next thing I knew, Dad had swung around with his fists and was only an inch from my face. It was terrifying to see his face turn so rigid and red. After he realized that he had come so close to hitting me, I saw tears in his eyes. He took me over to the side of the road and we sat on the bank. He explained how sorry he was, but that it was a natural instinct at the moment because of his nervous condition. Of course I didn't understand this at all. The only thing I knew for a fact was that Daddy had come home very different from when he had left to go off to the war.

Days passed and things began to seem more normal. I tried to be very quiet around the house so I would not frighten Daddy again. He wanted to go to his shop to see what was going on. Later I would discover that he had been so terrified of what he would find that he could not bring himself to go down to check on his business. But, he finally began to go to work and through the years that followed, he was successful in running one of the most reputable auto body shops in Columbia. It had been a long, difficult road for my Dad, but it had also been a road that had been a struggle for my Mother and brothers. Without the help and support of our friends and neighbors, we would not have made it through this very difficult time in our lives with all the adjustments each of us had to make. Through it all, I always knew that I was loved. I was cared for by my parents, my two brothers and my adopted second family that lived next door to us. Uncle Roscoe, Aunt Lula Mae, Vera, "Tootsie" and Sybil Byrd. The memories I have of each member of this wonderful family are etched in my mind *forever.*

The years that followed were some of the most fun times I remember. My family was happy again. We played and worshiped together. We owned a vacant lot next to our house. Dad and my brothers had turned it into a ball field so all the neighborhood kids could play ball with our parents on Saturday and Sunday afternoons. It seemed that we didn't have to have a great deal of toys to be entertained . . . we had each other and we enjoyed our times together with our friends and family. These were the 'good ole days,' before television took over our lives.

Mr. and Mrs. Wilson were neighbors who lived across the road from our community ball field. They had a parrot in a large cage they hung out on their front porch each day. It was so much fun to hear the parrot call the balls and strikes as we played ball. The parrot would mimic any conversation he heard. Aunt Lula Mae would come out to call her girls and the parrot would call each name as she heard Aunt Lula Mae call out for her girls. Each day when I came home from school, I would stop at the edge of the Wilson's yard and talk with their parrot. He could raise or lower his voice and it sounded just like he was having a conversation with you.

Chapter 6

MY YEARS GROWING UP

WHEN I WAS nine years old, we moved again. Dad bought a house that was only a little over a mile from where we lived at the time. It was on Two Notch Road. I made new friends, but I kept all my old neighborhood and church friends, we always stayed within a 1 to 2 mile radius each time we moved. I missed the Byrd neighbors, but we continued to visit and saw them at church each week.

Each year when time came to bake fruitcakes, Mother and Aunt Lula Mae would spend one whole day at our house cutting up fruit and nuts to bake cakes. The next day, they would spend the day baking the cakes. Our house smelled so good for days from the aroma of the fruitcakes baking. It was difficult to wait until the Thanksgiving and Christmas holidays before we were allowed to cut a cake. (That was the rule—no cake cutting before Thanksgiving Day dinner). Mother kept the cakes wrapped in a cloth in our glass front china cabinet in the dining room. In our house, you had to walk through our dining room from the kitchen to the rest of the house. I tell you, it was pure torture to smell the cakes everyday and not be able to taste them. Especially for the last two weeks before 'cutting day'. She would slice apples, paper thin and put on top of the cake, and pour a little wine over it to keep it moist. Honestly, this is a memory that I can still almost *smell*. They don't make fruitcakes like this anymore.

My years growing up were pretty normal, at least I didn't realize it if they weren't. I was happy and had many friends to pal around with. Mom and Dad had already instilled some good work ethics in me at an early age of ten. I actually had a job. I mowed the lawn and weeded the flowerbeds for my elderly neighbor next door. I used her old squeaky push mower to cut the grass, and pulled weeds down on my knees for what seemed like hours. I learned the art of making borders for flower beds by standing up brick at a 45 degree angle against each other. There really is an art to doing this. Especially when my neighbor wanted them to be *exactly* the same height.

I didn't work by the hour. This first job paid $2.50 for each mowing and weeding. It usually took me from 6-8 hours to complete the job. It was a *big* yard. With bathroom breaks, snack and rest breaks, I figured I was earning 42 cents per hour working six hours; and 31 cents an hour if it took me eight hours. Where, oh where were the 'child labor' advocates when I needed them? I learned a valuable lesson from this job though, . . . '*anything worth doing, is worth doing right the first time*', because if I didn't get the border brick going in a straight line *and* even, I had to start over. There was another benefit working with my neighbor. As we would sit and talk about what was going on in my life, little did I realize at the time just how much she was helping mold my life with so many of her long, philosophical stories. Some created many memories.

It was always more fun to follow my brother, David around and hang out with the neighborhood boys. Growing up with two older brothers made me enjoy doing things that boys did far more than playing with dolls. You could always find me wherever David was with his friends. Suffice it to say, as a kid growing up I would have been described as a 'Tom Boy' for sure. In spite of my love for pretty clothes, my comfort clothes were a worn out pair of dungarees, a long sleeve shirt with the tail of it pulled out, almost long enough to reach my knees. I would roll up one pants leg, sling it over my boys bike and follow David and his friends wherever they went. I can still hear David saying, "Sis, why don't you go home and play with your baby dolls?" It must have been pretty embarrassing for him to have a little sister tagging along with his friends.

I did have baby dolls. Each Christmas Santa would bring me a new doll. Some had extra clothes that you could change. The first thing I did was remove the clothes, maybe change them once, and then the doll was tossed aside, never to be played with again. What a disappointment I must have been to Mother at this stage in my life. Her only little girl, and the only type doll I was interested in was the sock, or rag dolls with the painted faces and yarn hair.

Boys Can Be Mean! (Even Brothers . . .)

One of the neighbor dads had put up a basketball goal on a vacant lot behind their house. To discourage my presence, the boys buried buckets of water along the basketball court and covered them with pine straw. They knew where these *booby traps* were buried and stayed away from them. But, when I showed up to play with them, they would always manage to throw the ball to me at just the right place so I would step in the bucket of water. Of course I would be furious, go home crying that they had made me get my jeans all wet. This would create hilarious laughter from the boys, my brother included.

The one prank that finally ended my wanting to hang out with the boys was the '*Swinging Pine Tree Game*'. The lot where the basketball court was located also had some small pine trees that you could climb up on. The object was to climb high enough to get the tree to bend down so you could hang like a monkey and ride the tree to the ground, push with your feet and ride the tree back up. It sure looked like fun to me. So one day while the boys were playing their pine tree game, I wanted to play. I should have known when they helped me climb the tree that their intent was 'evil'. They held the tree down and I climbed on. When they let go, being a light-weight, the tree flew up, rocked back and forth and I was hanging on for dear life. Boy was I scared. This game wasn't nearly as much fun as it appeared. They began hollering for me to just slide down the tree, which I did. The only thing that was wrong with the slide down was that I cleaned the tree trunk of the pine rosin with my jeans. Again, the hilarity broke out, I ran home bawling my head off only to have my Mom take the side of my brother and his friends. This was truly the last time I *ever* followed my brother and his *evil* friends. To this day I have *never* heard of anyone else playing this game.

Robert would take me with him downtown on Saturday nights to play the machines at the arcade that one of his friend's parents owned on Main Street in Columbia. He and his friends would take me to the movies with them. The movie theatre was right next door to the arcade. I'd have popcorn, candy bars and a drink. The movies were always a western with Cowboys and Indians. It's no wonder my movie hero was John Wayne. I think by the time I grew up I had seen all of his movies at least once.

As the years passed, Robert and David became more involved with their various jobs and friends. Their interests changed from playing mean tricks on me, to girls and cars. There weren't many girls in my neighborhood to play with. This is when my dad began to let me 'hang-out' with him

CHAPTER 7

MY BROTHER ROBERT was the first of my brothers to marry. He was only nineteen years old—but, he was a very *mature* nineteen year old. During the years Dad was away in service, Robert had taken on the role of being the 'father' figure in our family. Mother was twenty-nine when Dad left for the Navy, and Robert was thirteen—there was only sixteen years between their ages. He had already started working in my Dad's shop when he was in high school, so it was assumed he would continue when Daddy came home, which he did. His job was secure enough to support a wife, and he had certainly been exposed to what being the head of a family was like.

Robert married Bettie Gibbons. She was a lovely, petite, strawberry blonde, and a couple of years older than him. A year later, I became an 'aunt'. I was only eleven years old at the time and it was like I had acquired a BIG SISTER in Bettie, and a LITTLE SISTER when Carol was born. Carol was a real cutie. Mother kept her quite a lot when she was small and we became pretty close *buddies*. But, as I got older, she became sort of a *pest*.

Having been the 'baby girl' in my family, I think it gave me a sense of being over-possessive with my 'things'. I had a beautiful dresser in my bedroom. It had a bench where you could sit and look in the mirror while you put on your make-up, paint your nails or comb your hair. This bench had a very soft gold, velvety upholstery on the seat. It was just what a young girl loved in her bedroom. I kept all my rag dolls, and stuffed animals won at the fair, along my bed pillows at the tall headboard of my bed. I would come in from school, go to my room and immediately know that Carol was there, or had been in my room. My dresser would have nail polish all over it, including my pretty gold bench, and my 'stuff' on my bed would *not* be as I had left it. At the time I thought I had been lucky to have been the 'only little girl' in our house.

There was no question that I loved my niece though because as I finished school and went to work, I could not go shopping without buying at least one pretty little dress for Carol, which caused an embarrassing situation for me one Christmas.

I was dating a boy that year who was quite large, not fat, but he was 6' 5" and weighed 240 lbs. He had such a great sense of humor, that proved to be a real asset. Charlie and his family were from Georgetown, S.C. Each Christmas his family always spent the holidays together in Georgetown opening their Christmas presents.

On a Christmas shopping trip, I bought Charlie a beautiful hand knit pullover sweater. He was still in college and these were the style then. I also bought a pretty, very frilly little dress for my niece Carol. I wrapped my gifts after I got home and put them under our tree.

The week before Christmas, I gave Charlie his gift to take to Georgetown with his family. Robert and Bettie always had Mom, Dad and me over for Christmas breakfast so we could see Carol open her Santa gifts. We packed up on Christmas morning and went to Robert's with our gifts.

We began opening our presents. Carol went first. Of course she went for my gift first because it was the biggest one. When she opened the box, I was shocked! It was a beautiful light blue pullover sweater—large enough to wrap around her at least twice. "Oh NO," I exclaimed. I could only *imagine* Charlie opening his Christmas present in front of his family to find a size two pink, frilly dress. Even though we got a big laugh out-of-the mistake, I was so embarrassed I could just die.

Late that afternoon, the phone rang. It was Charlie calling from Georgetown. He was calm as could be when he said, "Jo Ann, I *love* the dress you gave me, but do you think I can get it in a *larger* size?" His family had also had a big laugh at my mistake. I am so careful now when wrapping gifts to be sure I have the right name tag on them. Charlie's sense of humor really paid off.

Carol has her own children, and grandchildren now, and when we get together we have such fun remembering all the fun we've shared over the years, very precious years. At Mother's graveside service, Carol stepped forward to pay her last tribute to my Mother, *her Grandmother*. She said, "I was Grandmother Doub's *first* grandchild. She had many more later, but, *I* had the privilege of being her very '*first*'. She made me feel so very 'special' when she called me 'Kay Kay', and I will always treasure the 'precious memories' of my life with her." When our family is together, I can't help but see how Carol is now making these *'forever memories'* for *her* grandchildren.

CHAPTER 8

WHEN I WAS nine years old, Saturdays were extra special for me. Daddy would let Mother sleep in. He and I would get up real early, go downtown and eat breakfast at his favorite café, the S & K on Hampton Street. Then we would take our usual trip to the Farmers' Market on Assembly Street in town. We would park his truck at his shop on Washington Street and walk up to the market on Assembly. He would start at one end of the market and walk every inch of the street where the vendors displayed their produce. It seemed like Dad knew every one of the vendors on the market. He would walk down the street, sampling the cheese, grapes, and tasting the watermelons the vendors had sliced. On our way back down the street, Dad would have sampled all the products he planned to buy that day. There was a vendor who had hot boiled peanuts. Daddy would stop at his stall first thing, sample one of the peanuts to see if they were salted just right. There were times I remember his telling the old man, "these peanuts got an extra shake of salt today didn't they?" No matter if they were too salty or not, we'd go home with a bag.

After we had finished our shopping on the market, before we went home, we would stop by Hiller Hardware Store on our way back to the shop. Dad knew all the people in *this* store too. He would go in, find a vacant keg, sit down and talk, talk, talk . . . I knew not to become whinny and ask him about going home. He would leave when they had finally solved all the world's problems that day. My entertainment during these long conversations was to browse around and look at all the fascinating things you could buy in the hardware store. To this day, I attribute my love for shopping in hardware stores to my hanging out with Daddy on Saturdays at Hiller's.

We would go home, sit on the front porch and eat our boiled peanuts. I never did acquire a taste for the wet slimy things. But, the companionship with my Dad was priceless. Mom was always happy to get the fresh vegetables and fruits we bought that day, and we usually had some of them included in our supper that night.

Summers after school was out were always exciting for me. Dad would take me with him to his body shop some days. He would set up some saw horses in back of the shop, give me some tools and sand paper and an old bent up car door or fender. I would work on that project all day getting it ready so he could paint it for me. Of course, this was not a part that would go back on a customer's car. He was just providing entertainment for me. I recall watching him work on a wrecked car that looked like it should be in the junk yard. After he had repaired the car, you could not find any indication that the vehicle had been damaged in an accident. Somehow his gift of restoring something broken to something useful again always fascinated me. There were times when he would give me extra allowance for my "hard work" at the shop. Daddy always had a wonderful way of making me feel special and loved. No matter what I did, if he saw me put my best efforts into it, regardless of the final results, he praised me for my work and determination. I wanted to make him proud of me, but it didn't take me long to know for sure that I didn't want to work on wrecked cars the rest of my life.

Self sufficiency was a quality Dad instilled in me and my brothers. If we needed, or wanted something done, we had to try to do it ourselves before asking someone else to do it for us. It wasn't that he wouldn't help us when we needed it, but we must first prove that we had at least made an effort on our own. Learning personal responsibility and accountability were two of the most valuable lessons my parents taught us. With me, it was almost to a fault that I learned this independence. After I married, my husband found this to be the most difficult trait dealing with my strong will and independence.

Not only did I have loving parents who taught me so many good values, but it was gratifying to have school teachers who taught me so much more than just reading, writing and arithmetic. They taught me discipline, self-worth, how to be independent and show respect for others. My school teachers were all an extension of my up-bringing at home by my parents. There was no question that my parents knew that I would be in capable hands when I was sent to school each day.

Many of my friends at the age of 14 or 15 made money baby sitting. This was never of interest to me, plus I didn't know many friends of my parents who had small children. I never had a baby sitter, other than my brothers, and there were very few occasions my parents left me with them. In those days, parents carried their children with them, or they stayed home with them. But, there was one specific occasion of being "baby-sat" by my younger brother David that will *forever* be remembered.

Mom and Dad had to attend the funeral of a relative in North Carolina during a weekday. I had to stay home to attend school. David was to take care of me.

Mother had worked for weeks re-painting our kitchen a bright yellow color. This was done with a brush using enamel paint. She was really proud of her efforts. This was only days before they had to make the trip to North Carolina for the funeral. I was 14 years old. David was the only one of my brothers who could cook. His specialties were opening a can of Campbell's vegetable soup, and he could make great pancakes, from scratch. Of course the only problem with his two specialties was that he would fix the vegetable soup for breakfast and the pancakes for supper. After two days of this same menu, I told him on the second evening, as he was preparing pancakes for supper, that I was **not** going to eat pancakes for supper anymore. Now David was a very good brother to me, but he did have a temper, so when I announced very emphatically that I was **not** going to eat pancakes again for supper, he turned around from the stove and threw the pancake utensil at me. I ducked to miss the flapper and it sailed across the top of the refrigerator and hit the freshly painted yellow wall of my Mom's kitchen, taking out a big portion of the paint and wallboard with it. Grease splattered on the wall and left marks. Well, I just stood there totally amazed that he could do so much damage with a pancake flapper. And, I could not wait until Mom and Dad came home later that night to show them just how "violent" David had been as my 'baby-sitter'.

I'm sure he realized just how much trouble he was in because he immediately cut the stove off, threw the pancakes in the trash, put me in the car and took me to the Varsity Drive Inn downtown for a hamburger, fries and a milkshake. I probably could have used this incident to even get a banana split. Of course, being the little 'bratty' sister I was, I still could not wait for Mother to see what he had done to her kitchen wall. The end of this story was that I was the one found to be at fault. (Who would have guessed?!)

I was reprimanded for not being *grateful* that he was even preparing me meals while they were away. I should not have "*provoked*" him. Lesson for me was that being '*unruly*', and '*ungrateful*' were not acceptable behavior tolerated by my parents. David did receive his punishment from Mom by having to re-paint the wall he had damaged. That was the last time I was left with a 'baby-sitter'.

I'm sure that my family was quite normal. David and I could fight like cats and dogs, but you let someone else say a harm word about one of us and we were like bantam hens jumping all over you to defend each other. I had learned very early that having two older brothers was indeed a real blessing to me. Back when David and his friends would be so cruel to me, and I would run home crying, later he would ride me on his bike up to the little community grocery store and buy me a popsicle. This was *after* his friends had left, of course.

Fair Week was always an anticipated event. School kids were given Fridays off to attend the SC State Fair. Daddy would always be very generous, giving me money to spend through the whole day. But, on Thursday night before the fair, Robert and David would come to me and ask if I had enough spending money for the fair. At this age, can you ever have **enough** money for the fair? I'd say, "Daddy gave me a *little* to spend." That wasn't exactly a lie! It was maybe hedging a little. I knew they'd both come through for me and I'd have much more money than I needed to be carrying around at the fair. I used to think that was what Big Brothers were for, *right?* After all, they had treated me badly at times. It wasn't considered '*lying*'. It was called '*payback*'.

Mother would take me and my friends down to the fairgrounds early on Friday morning and come back for us late in the afternoon. We would ride the carnival rides, at least twice. Eat at least one of everything they were selling in the food line. We would play all the chance games, win dishes, stuffed animals and trinkets. So many that we would be so tired from lugging all these winnings around, and so sick of the rides and junk food that we would be sitting by the entrance gate, waiting anxiously for Mom to come for us.

My teenage years were normal, at least I didn't realize it if they weren't. I was happy and had many friends to pal around with. Mom and Dad were very well aware of who my friends were. And, my friends were always welcomed into our home. Looking back, I can see that the purpose of this *open door policy* for my friends was so my parents could keep an eye on who I was choosing as friends. Mother used to say she never knew who was going to be sitting down at her table for a meal, because if a friend of my brothers, or mine, was at our house at mealtime, they were always invited to eat with our family. I sometimes wonder how she stretched five pork chops to feed two or three extra people. Remember the story in the Bible of the five barley loaves of bread and two fishes? When Jesus blessed it, they had enough to feed thousands, with baskets left over. It was a miracle! Dad's blessing of the pork chops must have worked too. We always had enough for friends. It was good Mother loved to cook. My friends thought she was the best cook in the community.

There were two young girls who lived about two blocks from us named Patricia and Joyce Rogers. I was the oldest of the three of us and we went through school together from elementary through high school. We were like sisters growing up. We played together, attended the same schools, and church with our families. Growing up, church was a vital part of our family and community life. 'Tricia, as I always called her, and Joyce had two older brothers named Hubert and Melvin, and they were friends with my two brothers. This family would become a major part of my life in later years.

CHAPTER 9

Turning 14—The MAGIC YEAR!
The Day I Got My Driver's License (Almost)

SINCE I GREW up with a parent in the automobile business, and two brothers who thought that a car was the greatest gift you received in this life, it was only natural that I learned about cars at an early age. You could get your driver's license at the age of 14. You could also get your Social Security Card at 14 to work. Actually driving was more fun at this age than working. Driving a car came as easy as falling off a log for me . . . it seemed natural. I used to ride in the cars with my parents, and my brothers. I'd watch every move they made with the brakes, clutch and accelerator. I'd watch their hand signals. In my mind I knew I could do it. Actually I started driving a car, (not legally), at the age of 12. David would let me drive his car on the back roads in the community. (This of course was without my parents knowledge.) Both brothers were very good drivers and taught me well.

When I was 13 in junior high school, they gave a driver's ed class. They had a simulated car setup in the classroom where you were tested on how you responded to various conditions and signs. When you had passed this test, they allowed you to take the written portion of the drivers' test. This is where my year of 'illegal' driving under the teaching of my brothers paid off. I passed both tests with flying colors. All I had to do was wait until I turned 14 to take the actual road test at the highway department.

The 'Big Day' came. My 14th birthday fell on a Saturday. This was perfect for Mother to take me for my driver's license. We took her car which was a big black Chrysler Imperial. It looked like a family funeral car. It was the only car in our family at the time that had an automatic transmission. Both my brothers had straight drive cars. And I did know how to drive them. Mom's car was one of the first that we owned with push button windows. I had practiced parallel parking which was one of the requirements on the road test. There was no question in my mind that I was going to get my driver's license on this *very special birthday.*

When we entered the Highway Department that day, I presented the certificate showing I had passed the written part of the test. I then was assigned to a patrolman who would give me the road test. Feeling pretty confident that I had nothing to fear, we proceeded to Mother's big black car for the test. As we drove out of the parking space, I rested my left arm on the big fat armrest, slung my right hand over the steering wheel and headed out to give this patrolman 'the ride of his life'.

The first words out of the patrolman's mouth were, "Take your arm off that armrest and put both hands on the steering wheel, who do you think you are, a racecar driver?" Now, not only was I startled at his gruffness, but I immediately thought,—to myself of course, 'now just who do *you* think *you* are telling me how to drive this car? I've been driving since I was 12 years old?' Well, we drove several more blocks and came to a side street around the University of South Carolina campus. It had a STOP sign so I came to a STOP. The street was also one that allowed diagonal parking along the side of the street which made me have to pull out just a little to be sure there were no cars approaching . . . this time I did not come to another complete STOP. The second words that came out of the patrolman's mouth were spoken even more abruptly when he said, "You just *rolled* a STOP sign lady." Now having passed my written test earlier, I could not recall anything about '*rolling* a STOP sign', but I'm sure it must have been in the book somewhere. Since he was completely in charge of this little venture, I did not open my mouth to his statement.

As, we approached the specified area where you parallel parked. I was *thinking to myself,* 'now you just watch how I put this big black funeral car in that little-bitty space', when he turned to me and said, "let's see what you can do with this?" I was truly thankful that power-steering had been in cars at this time, because I proceeded to adjust myself and was almost in the space when he said, "well, it's obvious you can park this thing, just pull out and head back to the station." I didn't even get the opportunity of showing him how I could accomplish this task.

We drove up to the curb where my Mother was waiting for me. I stopped the car, we got out and Mother asked, "Well, how did she do?" The grumpy old man looked at me and said, "I wouldn't ride with her another mile down the road. She *speeded* three times, *rolled* s STOP sign and drove like she thought she was a *racecar driver.*" I could see on Mother's face that she was stunned. Well, needless to say, this *special birthday* for me was the worst day of my life. I was going to have to admit to my friends that I had "failed" the driver's test. The very friends who had been riding in the same car with me for two years! But, it taught me one valuable lesson. You should never get the bright idea that you think you're the greatest driver in the world and be so confident that someone can't put you in your place. I'll never know just why he was so gruff and abrupt with me. But, I never to this day come to a STOP sign that I don't come to a full STOP. And I don't drive with my arm on the armrest. I won't use the term NEVER, but 99% of the time I have both hands on the steering wheel when driving. I don't recall having come to many STOP signs where the situation called for me to pull out to see oncoming cars, but you bet, if I ever do, I'll remember to come to a full STOP the second time before proceeding. I'll just bet you that I was not the first young person that he had failed on their first road test. I'm not sure the others learned the same lesson.

When you failed any portion of the driver's tests, you were required to wait one week before you could take the tests again. The next Saturday, after I had a week to *mature* my thinking a bit, Mother took me back for my second try for my license. On this day, I was assigned a younger patrolman for the road test. The first words he spoke to me were, "so you let the Patrolman scare you to death last week?" I did not respond. As we drove around for the test, he talked about his love for fishing and how he needed to be at the lake instead of working that day. We did not go the same route of the previous road test, but as we pulled up to the parallel parking space, he asked, "can you actually park this thing?" I did reply, with great confidence, "yes sir." "Well," he said, "let's get back to the office so I can get your license processed." When we got back to where Mom was waiting for me this time, I was so excited I pulled up to a "No Parking" space right in front of a fire hydrant. He just laughed and said, "Now young lady, you do know you can't park here!" When Mother asked him how I did this time he said, "She's a good little driver, in fact, I'd be willing to ride to California with her driving." WOW! Now that was the happiest day of my life. Heck, I must have really *improved* on my driving skills in one week.

Now, I cannot leave this part of my life without admitting to something that also had a profound mark on my life regarding my driving experience. The next day, on Sunday evening after attending church, a group of six girlfriends, ranging in age from 14 to 16, piled into my Mom's big black Chrysler to go for hamburgers at Doug Broome's Drive Inn on North Main Street.

This was 'the place to be' when you wanted to be seen with friends. As we were turning off Main Street on our way to the drive-in, some boys in another car began following us. I knew a back way to get to the drive-in so, in an effort to lose the car of boys following us, I quickly made a turn off Main Street. As I made the turn, the tires on the car squealed, just enough to attract a city policeman. I had to stop for a red light at the next intersection. When the light changed, I saw the lights on the patrol car start flickering, and he touched the siren lightly, just enough for me to know that I was his target. I crossed the intersection, which just happened to be the intersection of the junior high school I attended. I told the girls in the car to be very quiet. I must say that my knees were pretty shaky because it seemed to take him ages to get out of his car and approach my car window. The girls didn't help with their statement, "I think he's probably calling someone to take us to jail." When he finally came to the window, he asked to see my driver's license. I admit that I was embarrassed to let him know that they were only a little over 24 hours old. He left the car window, with my license, and went back to his patrol car, and I could see in the rearview mirror that he was on his radio. We waited, and waited. Finally he came back to the car and asked two questions: One, "Young lady, how old is the oldest girl in this car?", and the second question was, "Is your dad Lester Doub, the owner of D & D Body Shop?." The answer to the first question was 16, the answer to the second question was, yes he is.

The reason this experience made such an impact on my life so early in my driving career was that the lecture that followed my responses to the policeman made me feel so ashamed for two reasons. First, that I had abused the privilege my parents had given me by allowing me to drive such a nice car. And secondly, was the fact that I had put my friends in jeopardy by my irresponsible actions in the matter. The policeman said, "I'm not going to give you a ticket, BUT, I *am* going to tell your dad about this incident tonight." Oh Boy! I then began to beg him to write me a ticket. I thought that the very worst thing that could happen was for him to tell my Dad. At the time my Dad's garage was located on Washington Street in Columbia. It was less than one block from the City of Columbia Police Department. Many of the city policemen would hang-out at my Dad's shop. Some of them were the motorcycle cops. Many of them I had grown up knowing.

I knew that there was no way I could talk the policeman out of telling my Dad. I also knew that it was going to be 100 times worse on me if he learned of my careless driving from a city policeman. After we were allowed to drive away, the excitement of going to Doug Broome's Drive Inn for a burger was no longer on our minds. I asked my girlfriends in the car not to mention the incident to anyone. I didn't ask them to tell a lie, just not to mention anything at all. We all agreed. Case closed! I would wait patiently for my punishment from my Dad.

You know, it's amazing how your conscience can drive you crazy, when you try to keep something inside that you know in your heart should be dealt with and resolved. But the days and weeks went by with no mention by my Dad of this incident. Each evening when we sat at our supper table, our family always shared events with each other. Each time my Dad would say, "you know what?" when he began to tell something, my heart would almost stop. I just knew the policeman had carried through with his threat. Well, weeks went by with not a word. In fact, I had almost begun to stop thinking about the issue.

One day I came in from school, Mother was sitting at the kitchen table having her afternoon cup of coffee. She told me to put my books up and come into the kitchen that we needed to talk. I took my books to my room, went into the bathroom to brush my teeth, why I don't know. I brushed my hair and finally realized that there was no way to avoid the conversation waiting in the kitchen. When I walked into the kitchen, Mother told me to sit down. As I looked at her, I knew without any doubt that someone had squealed on me. She asked me first if what she had overheard in the grocery store that day was the truth about my being stopped by the policeman. That seemed so long ago now. But, I knew there was no way I was going to deny the fact. What I did want to know was *how* she had learned about it.

Seems she was sitting at the grocery store where she went almost each day for groceries, and her daily Coke and 'gossip' session, as Dad called it. One of the girlfriends in the car had told the grocery store owner's daughter about how we were pulled over by the cops. She had thought it was ironic that I had just passed my test the day before. My first thought was to be angry with my girlfriend for her breaking my confidence. My second thought was to thank her for finally getting the truth out so I could face the consequences and move on. The lesson for me was that you can harbor a lie, or deception, but your conscious will take away your peace. I was actually so thankful for the truth coming out. I had been trying to hide my feelings that, not only had I done a bad thing in my driving, but I had not been truthful with my parents. My Mom helped me follow through with clearing my conscious. She gave me the option of my telling Dad the whole truth at supper that night, or she would do the telling of how she had found out through her source at the grocery store. Well, it was one of the hardest things for me to admit to my Dad. He had been so gracious to me with allowing me privileges with his vehicles, without any reservations because he trusted me to act responsibly. I had broken this trust and I knew how disappointed in me he would be.

At supper that night, Daddy came home as usual. We were sitting at the table and I had lost my appetite just thinking how I was going to break this news. Finally, after Daddy had asked the blessing I said, "Daddy, I have something that I need to discuss with you." He said, "Okay Jo." I began to relate the entire incident and exactly how it had turned into a real nightmare for me. How it had lingered on my mind, affected my days concentrating in school, and how guilty I felt at not telling them the truth when it occurred. When I looked up, with tears streaming, I saw my Dad looking straight into my eyes as he said, "Jo, I knew the next morning after this happened what had taken place. I also knew that in time, you would have to tell me yourself." He said the policeman came by the shop the next morning, just as he had said he would, and told Dad about the Sunday evening traffic stop. He told my Dad that he wished he would not confront me about it to see if I would tell him myself what had happened. Daddy had kept this secret for all those weeks, and had not even shared it with my Mother. He was waiting for me to tell him myself.

You may be thinking this was an insignificant experience for me to have kept it in my memory for all that time. But, for me it was such a personal guilt I put on myself because of the love and confidence placed in me by my parents so early in my life regarding my driving. It reminds me of how important it is to follow your conscious when you know you should always be truthful and avoid losing the confidence of those who love you.

CHAPTER 10

A T THE AGE of nine I started taking piano lessons. Most of my teachers were members of my church. One was our church pianist, Mrs. Long, and she was fun. She could also play jazz and popular songs by ear. Before each piano lesson, she would sit at the piano and play some of my favorite songs for me. I always looked forward to going for my lessons with her. I was so amazed that she seemed to touch every key on the piano when she played. My second teacher, was the wife of our pastor. She was our church organist and did a great job, but during my piano lessons, she was always jumping up, taking care of her young son, or doing something in the kitchen. Both teachers lived close enough for me to ride my bike or walk for lessons.

My first year I learned to play pretty well. We had recitals at the church, attended mostly by family and church members. And, we were *always* allowed to use our music for the recital pieces. In junior high school I started taking piano from Columbia College. The very first day I showed up with my Baptist Hymnal, my teacher actually took it and threw it across the music room. It was the last time I saw that hymn book while taking lessons from her. Somehow I got the idea that this college music teacher didn't have the same appreciation for Baptist hymns as my first two teachers. She said, when she saw what I had been playing from, "We will NOT be using that book again. I'm going to teach you **music theory**." Heck, I didn't even know what **music theory** was. When it came to my recital, I didn't know that I was required to play my recital piece from memory . . . absolutely NO music allowed. These recitals were performed on the stage of the Columbia College Auditorium . . . In front of hundreds of people that I did not know. I had *always* been allowed to use my music before, and play in our church sanctuary for family and friends. This was one of my 'guardian angel moments' when I played in my *first*, and *last* recital at Columbia College. I never did progress much farther than playing hymns, but I did this very well. However, I couldn't play chop sticks without music notes in front of me.

I started playing the piano at church when I was 13 years old. I was never considered an accomplished musician . . . church hymns were my specialty. When I was 16 years old, our church was without a pastor, a music director and an organist. The Music Committee came to me and asked if I would consider playing the organ for church and our choir until they could find a new organist. Now at this time I didn't even know how to turn on the organ, much less play it for services. But, being too young to think there was something that I couldn't do, I said yes. So I would go to the church after school and practice until late in the evening every day. Some days I would be there 3 or 4 hours just practicing for the Sunday services. Time slipped away while I was practicing new sounds, because I could play as loud as I wanted to while no one was in the sanctuary.

Willie was the custodian of our church. He had been working in this capacity for as long as I could remember. When I went to the church to practice the organ, he would turn on the sanctuary lights just over the organ for me. He would stay close by while I was in the church alone practicing. You know, a church is a wonderful place to be with people in it, but it can be a scary building when you are there alone, especially in the late evening hours.

On one particular afternoon I dropped by the church to practice. Willie was no where in sight so I went inside, turned on enough lights for me to see the organ area and began practicing my music. I must have been entranced with my music when all of a sudden a black head rose up in our baptismal area above the choir loft . . . well, I was so frightened that I just dropped my arms on the organ keyboards and apparently my foot fell heavy on the volume pedal as the organ gave a loud blast throughout the church. Willie turned almost white and jumped out of the baptismal pool where he had been cleaning it. I said, "Willie, you just scared the life out of me," and he responded, "Lawdy, Miss Jo Ann, I thought when I heard that loud sound coming from that organ that the Lawd hisself done come down to git me." He never failed to let me know where he was after that little episode.

During my time playing the organ, I purchased a notebook form of the Baptist Hymnal. This three hole version allowed me the option of moving the music around so that I could coordinate with the church program without having to turn so many pages for the various congregation and choir specials. One Sunday morning the service had begun and we had sung our first hymn. Then we started into our second hymn of the morning. We began singing, and as I was reading the music several measures ahead, suddenly I realized that the hymn did not end at the end of that page. Well, as quickly as I saw this, my prayer went up to God, because I truly cannot play one note without the music in front of me. But to this day I do believe in miracles, because as we got to the end of the page, I continued to play the notes for the last line of the song, *without* any music. Now usually we Baptist are noted for singing the first and last stanzas of a hymn in church. Why I never know. Well there were three verses to the hymn we were singing, and on that Sunday we sang all three verses. I will forever remember the name of that hymn. It was "**To God Be The Glory**"! And each time we sang a new verse, I played the last line . . . *without* the music. Now that was my "quick answered prayer." That was the only time I wanted to play the *Amen* at the end of the hymn, even though we Baptist never sing the *AMENS* after our hymns. And I don't know why that is either.

The period during my organ playing in church was only for a few months, but those were the longest months I have lived through until this day. It was only because of my faith that God helped me accomplish this task. I found out that when you are young, you think there is nothing you can't do. You seem to have more nerve and will step out to take chances in life. The people of my church were all like relatives so they told me what a great job I was doing. I must have believed them, because our choir that year presented a Christmas Cantata and I was asked to play for one wedding. I wonder if that couple are still married. I can only hope their minds were on something other than the organ music I was playing that day. When I look back on this time in my life, it amazes me that I was either that brave or that stupid.

The absolute worst thing that happened during my temporary position as organist was the morning I was playing and the organ blew up. It began sounding like I was playing the wrong keys, which I did a lot, but this was *very* strange. There were sounds coming from that organ that I had never heard before . . . and I'm sure the congregation had not either. The choir members began looking at me, I suddenly realized that I should just turn the thing off and head for the piano to finish the rest of the service.

Years after this all happened, we would have many laughs about my experiences at the organ. When I think of what I put myself through, and the poor people who had to listen to my playing, it must have broken the hearts of the angels in heaven to have heard the sounds that came from our beautiful Baldwin organ for those few months. Only God could have taken the notes I played and turned them into beautiful music.

Chapter 11

During my four years spent at Columbia High School, I enjoyed some great times that created some wonderful memories for me. When I entered the ninth grade, I recall each time I gave my name, some of my teachers would immediately ask, "are you the sister of Robert or David?" By the tone of the teacher's voice I should have surmised that this wasn't exactly a 'positive' thing. Our last name was not a common, nor a familiar name to the area. We were the only family with this name in the Columbia area. It was a good old German name, DOUB. It was pronounced differently from the spelling. It was pronounced as Dabb. It was a sure thing that I indeed was related to those two 'notorious' brothers who had gone before me. As the years passed, I hope I helped change the impression left by my two older brothers who had graduated earlier from CHS. I always told Robert and David that they were a 'hard act to follow'.

... *A Romance Blossoms* ...

When I was in the eleventh grade, I began to learn how to ride horseback. I had several friends who owned horses and I was privileged to be able to enjoy riding, without the expense, or trouble of caring for them. This became a real enjoyable hobby for me in the afternoons after school and on weekends. It also presented me with an opportunity to meet, and fall in love with a young horseman. He had already finished school and was working as an electrician. Although I had enjoyed dating during my high school days, I knew this was a '*forever*' kind of love. So, as I fell in love with the horseback riding hobby, I also fell madly in love with this dashing 'horseman' named Donald.

We began dating during my junior year and into my senior year of high school. During this time his mother was the manager of the S & H Green Stamp store located on Main Street in Columbia. She gave me a job working on weekends and holidays. This was such a fun job that I think I would have worked there even if she hadn't paid me. Green Stamps were given by some merchants for purchases of groceries and gasoline mostly. You put them in little books and each book was valued at $3.00 for redemption at the Green Stamp Store for merchandise. Christmas was such a fun time. The little kids would come in with their one book of stamps, and almost all of them wanted to redeem the stamps for a pair or roller skates. Then there were some ladies who would come in with grocery bags full of books of stamps. They would actually save up their stamps and do their Christmas shopping. The merchandise was very nice quality, and it was the most fun job I ever had.

On my seventeenth birthday, and my last year of high school, Donald gave me a beautiful diamond engagement ring and asked me to marry him. It was one of the happiest days of my life. When I went home that evening and woke my parents to announce the news that I would be getting married, it didn't turn out exactly as a happy ending for the evening's event. My dad actually cried, real tears. I could not understand why. Later he explained that it had nothing to do with Donald. In fact my family considered him to be a very fine person, and loved him dearly. Dad just thought that I was too young to make this decision, not even having graduated from high school. It also made him realize that he would be losing his 'little girl' to some other man. I guess I had always thought that when the time came for me to leave home when I married, that my parents would be rejoicing to have an 'empty nest'.

As time would soon tell, apparently my first real love was not to be a *'forever'* relationship. Our interests and friends soon began to separate us from our commitment to each other. As the saying goes, 'the first real love is never forgotten'. A broken heart takes time to heal. It leaves a *precious memory* that only time can erase. And, not only did I feel a loss for Donald, but I loved his mother and three sisters as well.

Graduation from high school finally came in May of 1956. I was 17 years old. Did not know what I would do with the rest of my life yet, so I worked at Southern Bell Telephone Company during the summer that year. It was only a temporary job, but working on special projects making over-time, I had more money than I knew what to do with. I was still living at home, had no expenses, and all this cash was beginning to turn my head away from entering college, or nursing school. I had to make a choice of what I would do. My parents had already said they would pay my tuition for either choice I made.

In high school I had taken all the academic courses preparing me for college. I had also taken some extra courses in business, shorthand, typing, and bookkeeping and had done well in each of these subjects. But, I had not yet decided what I wanted to do when I graduated.

Opportunities for women in the 1950's after graduating from high school were not as open to girls. Some of my friends went on to college to become teachers, or some other special career choice, and a few went on to college to major in *"matrimony."* High school graduates were pretty much limited to working with the largest employers such as, Southern Bell, SC Electric & Gas Company or one of the local banks. Somehow none of these jobs seemed attractive to me.

At this point in my life I now realized that I *was too young* to get married and begin having a family. But, I did not have a clear picture of where I was to fit into this world. How I could use the knowledge gained from my school years, and in a place where I could benefit myself, and others. On a particular Sunday morning, I listened to my pastor give a sermon on "Making The Right Choices In Life." His sermon was based on the Bible Scripture found in **Jeremiah 29:11 NIV**

> *"For I know the plans I have for you,"*
> *declares the Lord, plans to prosper you and*
> *not to harm you, plans to give you hope and a*
> *future."*

That scripture, and the sermon I heard that day helped me make my choice. I finally decided that I would find a permanent job. After making the decision not to go to college, I remember using the fact that my Mother and Dad had not even finished high school as my argument for not needing to go to college. In fact, the most impressive fact about my parents was that Dad only had a seventh grade education, and Mother only went through the third grade in school. It was always amazing to me how my Dad had such knowledge, and was so successful in starting his own business with so little formal education.

I can recall times in my high school years that I would be studying my English lessons. I would come across a word that I did not know the meaning of and would ask my Dad what it meant. He not only could give me the meaning of the word, he would spell it for me. Sometimes I wouldn't believe him and would get my Webster's Dictionary down and look up the word.

And you know what? He was right every time. He was also very good with figures and could help me with my math homework. I remember his reading a lot. He always kept his Bible next to his chair and every evening he would read for at least an hour before he would pick up the afternoon newspaper. In those days I wondered why he would read from a book that was such 'old news' before he read the 'current news'. I know now that it was because he had his priorities in the right place.

Mother was really the most amazing of the two though. With her third grade education, she could read and write and her grammar was much better than some of my friend's parents who were college graduates. None of my friends ever believed it when I would actually brag about my Mother and how she was such a *'refined woman'* with such a limited formal education. She was one of the most elegant ladies I have ever known. She brought sunshine into the lives of every one she met. Our house was always open to our friends. It was because Mom and Dad loved, and enjoyed being with their kids.

In the fall of 1956, I went to work for Dreher Packing Company, a local meat packing company. It was a small family owned business and I enjoyed working in the office. The Personnel Manager was also the Vice President of Finance/Accounting. He immediately took me under his tutorage in the field of accounting and spent extra time teaching me accounting. I had taken some basic business skills in school, but I needed training in the specific job I was hired for. I always felt that I had received the equivalent of a four year college education while being taught by Mr. George Ramsey. He always used his knowledge and great patience in his teaching me general accounting. In fact, Mr. Ramsey made the field of accounting so interesting for me that I decided to stay with this company for 15 ½ years. I was the first woman to be given a management level position.

CHAPTER 12

My "<u>Forever</u>" Love Story

T HE SPRING OF 1959 was the beginning of a very interesting year in my life. It had been quite a few years since I had seen the older brother of my friends, Tricia and Joyce Rogers. Hubert had been friends with my brother David, and my memories of him had become a bit faded. He used to come to our house often when he and David would go fishing, or play ball together on our church softball team. My most vivid recollection of him was that he always liked to pull my pigtails when he was around me.

Hubert had gone to work for Southern Bell Telephone Company after graduating from high school, and was drafted into the Korean War at the age of twenty. I remember Tricia and Joyce talking about his being away in service, but I was only ten years old at the time. When he came home from the War, he went back to his job at Southern Bell and worked out-of-town most of the time. Our paths just never crossed again until one evening while I was visiting his sisters. Hubert was at home that night, and as I passed by his room, I saw him sitting on his bed cleaning his shotgun. I stuck my head in the door and we talked briefly. It was almost like I was seeing him for the very first time. Suddenly we didn't look at each other in the same light. He wasn't the same person that found delight in pulling my pigtails years ago, and I wasn't the pesky little sister of his friend, David. Those ten years difference in our ages didn't seem so far apart.

After our happenstance meeting again, I didn't seem to get Hubert off my mind. At the time I was going with a boy who was in college at Clemson. Although our relationship was not that serious, neither of us was dating any one else. Actually, Bob was the next door neighbor of Mr. George Ramsey, my boss at Dreher Packing Company where I worked. The one problem with our relationship was that I was working in Columbia, and Bob was in school at Clemson. He did not come home every weekend because of his involvement with various activities at school, so this left me with some free time, especially when I was not going up to Clemson for ballgames or other events.

It was in April of '59 when a business sorority that I belonged to, Beta Sigma Phi, was having a cook-out at Lake Murray. I had asked Bob to come home for this weekend, but he was having final exams and had to stay at school and study. This posed a problem, because in those days, girls just didn't attend dances or outings without a date. I still had my girlfriend's brother, Hubert in my mind, but I had not told either of his sisters of this. Even though we shared most everything with each other, I knew they would think I was out-of-my mind.

Tricia and Joyce picked me up to attend choir practice on Wednesday evening. They knew that I was planning to go to the party at the lake on Saturday. I just said to them, "Bob can't come home for the party on Saturday, so I was thinking about asking Hubert to go with me. What do you think?" They both just laughed and said, very emphatically, "NO WAY! He is a 'confirmed bachelor', and happy to be one." I was so intimidated by their response, and I think a bit challenged by it as well. I knew my work was cut out for me, if I pursued this thought.

The next morning at breakfast, I asked Mother, "Mom, do you think I should ask Hubert to go with me to the cook-out this weekend since Bob can't come home?" Mother said, "Hubert who?" I was flabbergasted that she did not seem to know who I was talking about. He had hung out at our house over the years with David, she had treated him like a son. She even sent him cards and letters while he was in Korea during the war, and was so excited when he finally came home. And she was now asking me, "Hubert who!" Then she said, "well, you know he's too old for you, he's your brother's age." I told her that this was exactly why I wanted to ask him to go with me to the lake. I felt very safe with him and I knew he would be a lot of fun and fit in very well with the people who would be there. Mother then said, "well, I'll tell you one thing, you could not be with any one that I would like more than Hubert." That did it!

He had a big, fast ski boat, drove a convertible and was quite a good looking guy. I would be very proud to have him *escort* me to the party.

My plan was to call him and just casually mention that I needed someone to take me to the lake on Saturday. This was on Thursday night when I called him. We talked for a long time on the phone. We laughed. Each of us sharing memories of things that had happened when he was friends with my brothers. Times he had tantalized me by pulling my long pigtails. How he remembered seeing me at his house several weeks earlier, and how he had entertained the thought that I had finally grown up. I was no longer the pesky little sister of his friends David and Robert.

I finally got around to asking him if he'd like to go with me to the cook-out at the lake on Saturday night. He hesitated a bit then said, "Well, I've already made plans to go on a weekend fishing trip to our house at Santee with some friends, but I'll think about it and get back to you." At this time my little heart was just about to beat out of me with excitement. I had at least gotten to first base in this quest for a date with Hubert. The game wasn't won yet, but I hadn't heard the "NO WAY" come from him like his sisters had said.

The next day I went to work. When I walked in the house that afternoon, Mom announced that Hubert had called and would call back later. I didn't know whether to be excited or disappointed about his call. So I waited, and waited, and waited . . . by the phone. When he finally called, I answered the phone very casually, trying to hide either excitement of disappointment. We talked a little about what kind of day we each had had at work, and then he said, "I have talked with my buddies about the fishing trip this weekend, and we've decided to go another time, so I can go with you to the lake." I told him how sorry I was to have made him change his plans, since I knew how much he loved to fish. (Boy did I lie!) I then gave him all the details of the time and plans for the party. He truly seemed interested. WOW!!!! That was on Friday. I think Mother was just as excited as I was. She then said, "now Jo, you know you're going to make Bob pretty angry about taking someone else. You should consider how it will look to him." She was really putting me on a 'guilt trip'.

I somehow had gotten so excited about the prospect of proving my friends wrong about their brother Hubert, and their statement of 'NO WAY would he go with me', that I had forgotten about Bob at Clemson. First I had to call Tricia and Joyce and let them know they didn't know their brother very well, and they certainly didn't put much faith in my charm. Then I had to place a call to Bob at Clemson to verify that it would be O.K. with him if I was being *escorted* to the cook-out on Saturday by the 'older' brother of my closest friends.

The first call made was to Hubert's sisters. It was one I was looking forward to. I always hated losing a fight about something, and most definitely had taken their response as a real challenge, and had WON! Joyce said, "he won't go, he'll find a way to get out of it." Another challenge and lack of confidence in me. It appeared they didn't want me to get involved with their brother.

The second call I made didn't turn out to be quite so pleasant either. Bob was very disappointed that I could think so little of *him* and his dedication to stay at school and study for his finals. I couldn't believe he was being so inconsiderate of *me* over this *'escort'* date. I clearly could not see what the big deal was about it. After all, it could not turn into anything serious . . . NO WAY! I finally ended my phone conversation with Bob by explaining that I only wanted to attend the big party and could certainly not go alone. He promised to come home the next weekend and we'd continue this discussion.

Saturday night came . . . finally! I couldn't remember a time when I had felt so excited about going out with anyone in a very long time. I changed my outfit, at least a dozen times. At first I thought that I should look like Hubert's younger sisters . . . then I changed my mind. I decided that I should dress a little *'older'* than his sisters, since he was so much older than me. *Then,* I changed my mind again. Finally, mother came into my bedroom, saw all the clothes scattered all over the chair, bed and floor and said, "Why don't you just dress for your age and begin to ACT your age? After all, he's just going to be your 'escort' for this one evening." That did it. I hung up all my clothes, put on my jeans and a blouse that I would wear if I was going to the lake with my parents.

When the time came for Hubert to pick me up, I was pretty calm and looking forward to an evening reminiscing about old times growing up around him and my brothers. That was pretty much our conversation the whole evening. We had a great time together. My friends fell in love with him, and of course his bright and shiny new white convertible didn't go unnoticed.

On the way home, he had put the top up on his convertible, turned the radio to some nice listening music, and somehow the evening didn't remind me anymore of the same 'old times' growing up with him and my two brothers. It had turned into something more meaningful for me. Some time during the evening while we were enjoying ourselves at the party, he had looked at me and seen that I was no longer the little pigtailed menace sister of his friends. And, I had looked at him, not as just my 'big-brother escort' for the evening. I still felt safe. But I now had a feeling of excitement and anticipation towards him as our conversation became more personal.

Of course the conversation was pretty straightforward. One statement he made, which quickly led me to believe that he wanted to set the record straight between us was, "I don't know about you, but I don't believe in marriage." At the time he was 31 years old and I was 21. I could truthfully agree with him on this statement. It brought back the conversation I had with his sisters when I first mentioned his going with me to the party. They knew his feelings about getting married. But my goodness, this was only a one time occasion, I wasn't planning on asking him to marry me, at least not *tonight*.

As we arrived home, we expressed our feelings about the fun evening we had. I thanked him for changing his plans to take me to the party, we got out of the car, he walked me to the door, we said our goodnights, . . . and the evening ended.

Mom was still up. She came into my room and asked how the party went. I recall asking her, "Mom, do you actually think 10 years is too much difference in age for a girl and boy?" As always, Mother gave much thought to her answers to my questions. She just looked at me with a big smile and said, "and did you forget that there are 10 years difference between your Dad and me?" They had run away and gotten married when she was 15 years old because her mother had not approved of the age difference between them. That was the only answer I needed to hear. I knew Mother had approved of my going out with Hubert. She had loved him like a son during the years he had spent hanging out at our house with my brothers.

On Sunday morning I went to Sunday School. I could not wait to face Hubert's sisters to let them know how *wrong* they had been about their brother. And, how successful I had been in my quest. When I got home after church that day, I received a phone call from Hubert. He said he was going back up to the lake to take his boat and have a cook out with a couple of his friends that evening. He asked if I'd like to go with him. WOW! I felt like I had really won BIG TIME! When he came to pick me up in his bright, shiny white convertible, with the top down and pulling his big bright, shiny new boat behind it . . . I was impressed!

When we arrived at the lake where he was meeting his friends, they were pretty surprised that he had brought a "date." The girl said he came up very often to ski and fish with her husband, but this was the first time he had ever brought a date. It made me feel pretty special. The day was such fun. We rode around in the boat but the water was still too cool for waterskiing. I'm not sure at what moment I got this funny feeling that I could really fall for this guy. He was not treating me like a 'little sister' anymore. He was very attentive to me, treating me like I was pretty special. We enjoyed the day and after our cook-out we walked down to the dock to continue our conversation . . . alone. This was the first time I had ever dated anyone 10 years older than me. I found myself trying to be grown-up and overcoming my self consciousness of his being the brother of my friends. It finally occurred to me that I should just 'act like myself.'

As we sat for a long time in silence just looking at the moon's reflection on the water, something happened to my heart. I felt that our being together was so natural. Like I had been waiting for him all my life. Reality told me that this would probably not go any further towards anything romantic. Especially since he had told me very emphatically the night before that he didn't believe in marriage. It was almost like I was preparing myself for another '*heart-break*'. Marriage was not my immediate goal. Hubert was someone that I thought I could enjoy dating. We had a good time together.

After saying our goodbyes to his friends we left. On our drive home I had the shock of my life. Hubert said, "Jo Ann, I have a confession to make. The night I saw you at my house when you were visiting Tricia and Joyce, I could not get you off my mind. I've been thinking about calling you to see if you'd like to go out for dinner and a movie." My thought was, 'how could this be happening in such a brief time?' Of course the years that I had been around him made it anything but a momentary meeting. He knew me, my family and it was the same for me. Our families had been intertwined for many years. We were neighbors, we went to the same church and although the difference in age kept us apart during school years, we still had a bond that seemed to be much more than a casual acquaintance. He knew me. He knew my family.

Two weeks went by. I was seeing, and talking more frequently with Hubert. Bob finally came home from Clemson and we had a date on a Saturday night. Now Bob did not have excess money to spend on dinner at fancy restaurants. He had to be very conservative with his cash, so we were back to the movies and sharing a box of popcorn. But this date was to be a very important time together. During the evening our conversation was mostly about school, his studies and looking forward to his coming home for the summer where he had a job waiting for him. The time came that we had to address the subject of my taking someone else to the party. I knew Bob's feelings about not 'wanting to share' his girlfriend. It wasn't that I did not care deeply for Bob. We had shared some great times together. He was a person who had high goals set for himself and he had the potential for meeting each one of them. I knew in my heart that what I had done by inviting Hubert to go with me to the cook-out was not something Bob would smile upon. I now realized that it had been a very selfish thing for me to do.

As we talked during the evening, each of us shared our deep feelings for each other. We rationalized how our continuous dating wasn't going to work. Bob had two more years at Clemson. We had never addressed the subject of our getting married. And although we shared a mutual respect and attraction for each other, we had to admit that our being separated for at least the better part of nine months while he was at Clemson, and I was working in Columbia, that our lives were going to require each of us to make a serious commitment for our relationship to continue. I had spent many days trying to determine if what we shared was solid enough for me to give up some of the fun and activities that I would be included in while he was away at school. Considering what had been on my mind, and my heart since Hubert had been brought into the picture, I finally decided that it was not fair to Bob to continue the relationship. It was a difficult decision to make, I think for both of us, but we were mature enough to break-up the relationship while we could still continue to be friends.

I had always felt that a close friendship should be the best foundation for a romantic relationship. This was what had transpired between Hubert and I in this brief time. I could almost feel that we had found a true friendship that was going to lead to something beautiful. It had gone beyond my sharing my emotions with his sisters. It had gotten 'personal' to me.

Our first event together was in the middle of April. From that time we began to see each other more frequently. He took me to dinner at the finest restaurants, concerts, the movies, and water-skiing at the lake during the summer. This was so contrary to the college and high school boys I had dated. He played on the company baseball team. I would go with him to his games, sit in the stands and feel so proud to be his date.

By the end of the summer of '59, he had discovered that he wasn't such a 'confirmed bachelor' after all. We continued dating during the fall and winter of '59. On July 21st of 1960, Hubert proposed marriage with a beautiful diamond engagement ring. This came as a great surprise to me. We had discussed marriage, but it was always someone else's marital status. There were times when his comments regarding being married led me to believe that he probably was satisfied with his freedom. He had seen quite a lot of unhappy marriages with friends who had already been married, had children and had gone through very nasty divorces.

I knew that he had pondered this decision about marriage with much resistance, before finally admitting that he wanted to be a devoted husband and begin a family together.

Hubert had said, "now I don't want a *big* wedding and I don't want to wait *too* long before we get married." So we began making our plans. Of course with me being my Daddy's 'baby girl,' and the *only* girl, I knew there would be a formal wedding in the church. After all, both my brothers had been married in our church and both of them had very big weddings. In fact, the year my brother David got married, it was on the hottest day in July that year, and the air conditioning had gone out in our church just before the wedding. I remember as a bridesmaid in a long gown, I could feel the perspiration run down my legs into my shoes. Mother had said to Hubert at the reception that she surely hoped that he would plan to get married on a cooler day. Hubert had said, "Mrs. Doub, you can be sure that when I get married, it will be a cold day in hell." Never did he dream that he would indeed be getting married some years later, especially to her daughter.

Our wedding took place on November 18, 1960, in Crescent Hill Baptist Church in Columbia where we had both attended all our lives. He had his wish that we would not wait so long to be married. It was four months after we became engaged. It was a beautiful wedding, not very small though as Hubert had requested. I had five bridesmaids, one junior bridesmaid, a flower girl and ring-bearer. He had five groomsmen, and his brother was his best man. Although my *'dream wedding'* had been to get married at Christmas and use red and white. November was close enough. It was a beautiful 'red and white wedding'. The November day was just perfect for a fall wedding. Not *cold* as he had told my mother it would be, but very pleasant. We spent a week in Florida on our honeymoon before we came home to live in our new home in West Columbia.

I remember each time we discussed the wedding plans, Hubert would say, "now Jo Ann, I don't want this to be a BIG wedding." He was so concerned that he would be too nervous to walk down the aisle, and not be able to say wedding vows in front of hundreds of people. But, he survived, he was as polished as a politician and enjoyed every minute of the event. It truly was a 'family affair'. There were my two brothers, and a niece of mine, his two sisters, and his younger brother, his Dad, and his nephew were all in the wedding party. It was as if God had planned this wedding even as far back as when Hubert was pulling my pigtails as a child. Love is so strange. No one believed that Hubert would ever get married. Least of all, ME!

Our life together was good. Hubert had bought our house before we got married. We were both established in good jobs. We traveled all over the United States, by car of course. Hubert had a fear of flying. And as I would learn in later years, this fear was truly a frightening phobia of his. Eventually he did conquer this fear enough times for us to travel to many parts of the world. Hubert was the best at planning trips. He would have made a wonderful travel agent. For months before a trip, he would research everything we should see and do in places we traveled to. His love of history and reading made him perfect for planning trips.

We would leave home on a road trip, and he would leave an itinerary for our family. It would give them the approximate number of miles we planned to travel each day, and the location with phone numbers where we could be reached in the evenings. This was before cell phones. He would have laid out plans for us to see everything interesting and historic in each state and city we traveled in the United States, Canada and Mexico. Our hotel reservations were made in advance for each trip, and I never remember but one occasion where we had to change these reservations.

It was a hotel out West that advertised as '*The City's Most Famous and Historic Hotel located in the Heart of the City*'. They were absolutely right in their advertisement. It *was* and old hotel, that should have been demolished years before. It *was* located in the heart of town, just not the most *desirable* part. When we arrived there late in the afternoon, we parked on the street in front of the hotel. I noticed several scantily dressed '*ladies*' standing by the entrance to the hotel. Hubert went inside to register. He wasn't in there five minutes when he came out with a strange look on his face. Seems he had booked us into the city's '*most famous brothel*'—and it wasn't cheap! We moved on to another town before we stopped for the night. We had a big laugh about this experience. Hubert was a very articulate person. He took care of the smallest details, and worried about many things that would never happen. He wanted to be prepared if they did. This is how he lived every phase of his life. It was either in memories of the *Past*, or the anticipation of the *Future* . . . Truth being, neither of these were areas he could change.

The one thing that was missing in our lives was that we did not have children. There were times when we considered adopting, but there always seemed to be some questions in our minds about this. The only thing that prevented us from being a near perfect couple, was that he was not a professing Christian. Hubert had been brought up in the church, in fact his mother was almost a fanatic about religion. If her children didn't go to church every time the doors opened, they could not participate in any other function or activity. This was true for all her four children. It must have made some negative impact on Hubert's life, because it was not until he was 40 years old that he made a decision in his life to accept Christ as his Savior, and was baptized into the Baptist church. I felt that God had answered my years of praying that Hubert would become a Christian. I never accepted his mother's advice when we became engaged. She had called me one morning to tell me that she loved her son but, he was not a Christian and she would prefer that I not marry him until he did make this decision in his life. My answer to her was, "I too love your son, as God does. I will not give up on him, just as God will not close the door on him. And I *will* marry him"

It was a similar story that Mrs. Rogers had put her son, Melvin and his wife Eugenia through when they announced that they were going to be married. She had said they were too young. And, there were some who would agree that 18 and 19 year olds are quite young to take on responsibilities of married life. Melvin and Eugenia had dated several years. Their intentions were always to be married as soon as they finished high school. They actually got married a short time before Hubert was discharged from service. Mrs. Rogers had thought she could get Hubert involved with talking Melvin out of marrying so young. It didn't work. They married. Had two children, a boy and a girl. Melvin went to work with Southern Bell and retired from AT& T several years ago. They are still together after 58 years and are as happy today as they were as teenagers. They have several grand, and great-grand children who are their treasures.

Tricia, Hubert's older sister was almost 'banned' from the family because she married a 'Catholic', rather than a *Baptist*. Joyce, the youngest, married a divorced man with a young child. This was not acceptable to their mother's plans for their lives. It was hard for me to accept a mother-in-law who could not be happy with the choices *any* of her children made for spouses.

CHAPTER 13

A s every child of God knows, Christians are not exempt from problems. God's Word tells us this in Psalms 34:18-19.

> '*The Lord is close to those whose hearts are breaking;*
> *He rescues those who are humbly sorry for their sins.*
> *The good man does not escape all troubles—he has them too.*
> *But the Lord helps him in each and every one.*'

It was in the spring of 1965 when Hubert and I decided to build a new home. Things were going well for us . . . or so I thought. Because he was such a very quiet person and kept so many thoughts to himself, I did not realize that he was entering into a state of depression. I had never experienced depression in my family, and did not recognize the illness until it materialized in a very bad way. Hubert became withdrawn from family, and friends, and gave up a lot of the activities he enjoyed. To him, it was a very disgraceful thing to admit that he could not control his feeling of depression. With medication, and determination on his part, he was able to overcome this bout with depression.

Mother and Daddy had a small cabin on Lake Murray. **Small** meaning one very large room, a one person kitchen at the end of the room, and a bathroom divided by a curtain on a rod over the door. It had provided many over-night gatherings for our family, with pallets spread over every inch of the floor. When you woke up in the mornings, you never knew whose child had crawled into your pallet during the night. We used to say you had to take a number to use the bathroom . . . and if you liked privacy, this was *not* the place to stay over-night. But what fun we had. Dad taught most of my friends to water-ski during those years. Mom and Dad loved to fish, but when Lake Murray started building up, and the water skiing became popular, Dad said the fishing there was no fun anymore.

So, in 1965, the same year we began building our house, Dad leased a lot from Santee Cooper on Lake Marion. With the help of Mother, and Hubert, he cleared the lot and prepared to build a cabin on it. Dad bought all the materials from an old house that was being torn down in Columbia, hauled the materials to the lake and began putting his building plan together. Dad was an automobile body man. He wasn't a carpenter. He had no house plans, just a mental picture and a sketch on a piece of notebook paper. What he did have was his desire to have a lake cabin so he and Mom would have a place to go fishing. He also had a brilliant mind for figuring numbers. He would look at his measurements and figure how many concrete block he needed, how much lumber he would need and the tools necessary to put it all together. He would head out for Holly Hill and come home and begin his building. Dad had made friends with a Negro family who lived not far from where he was building. They had several sons. The father had told Dad that Willie, his 10 year old boy was very good at building and could probably help him some.

Dad finished their cabin the latter part of 1965. I could not believe what a nice job he had done on this cabin. He had built it with materials that had come from an old house, the windows, doors and the beautiful hardwood floors were all included in the deal. It was the cutest little place, screened porch on the lakeside and a perfect setting back in a small private cove. He also built a long pier and boat dock where Mom could sit on and fish all day. Dad used to say after they finished the cabin that he was the 'architect' and Willie was the 'general contractor'. Later, Dad and Willie added on another room. Over the years, Willie continued to be my Mom and Dad's 'right-hand man'. When he graduated from high school, he went to work with one of the largest construction companies in that area. He always said his ability for carpentry came from Dad's teaching him the trade. *And . . . my Dad only had a 7ᵗʰ grade formal education.* I think he was blessed with many natural abilities.

I relate this story because, at the time when we were building our new house, and Hubert had begun to go through these periods of depression, the project that Dad had at Santee with clearing his lot and building the cabin was a diversion for him. He was always the happiest when he was busy doing something with his hands. I used to tell him that I didn't think his mind ever slept.

My Dad and Hubert were dear friends. They had a deep relationship, along with being in-laws in life. They fished and hunted together. One of my fondest memories of the two of them related to some hunting dogs.

Hubert and I made a trip to Winston-Salem, NC one weekend to buy a pair of Blue Tick Beagle puppies for he and Dad to train as rabbit dogs. The dogs were bred by my Uncle John whose specialty was this breed of Beagles. There were six puppies in the litter. When we got ready to load up the puppies for the trip home, Hubert ask Uncle John what he planned to do with the rest of the litter. Uncle John said he had a friend who had been waiting for a litter. I never knew what transaction transpired between Hubert and my Uncle John, but when we got in the car . . . there were six little Beagle puppies in the backseat. Hubert had built a special pen for the puppies to travel in. It covered the backseat of the car.

We decided that we needed to stop in Charlotte to let the puppies out to 'take a rest stop'. The filling station was off the highway a little ways and there was a picnic table where we could sit and have a snack while the little ones took care of their business. I never knew eight week old puppies with very short legs could run so fast. I looked around and they had scattered under the picnic table, under the car, under a large dumpster. We were on our hands and knees rounding up these six little rascals. They were the prettiest little butterballs who could outrun a Greyhound. When we got home, the problem got even worse. The pen and dog house Hubert had built was not large enough to house six puppies. It was built off the ground, had flooring in it that could be hosed down. The roof was shingled and it had bedding inside that was nice and cozy.

Hubert immediately called my Dad with the news that he'd better get busy building a doghouse at the lake so the little ones would have 'comfort' when they came to stay with him. Dad had said he would keep them and begin training them for rabbit dogs. Dad loved rabbit hunting, and he loved his dogs. This was a perfect set-up. At least it seemed to be perfect.

The only thing that Hubert had not thought of, especially when his purchase of two puppies had grown to six, was that they loved to dig. We arrived home around lunch time on Sunday. It took us the rest of the afternoon getting our 'new family' settled in. We were both exhausted, and hungry. We hadn't eaten anything since our little snack in Charlotte, and we had already expended our energy from that food chasing the puppies. Everything seemed to be settling down so I fixed a little supper for us. We were sitting at the table eating, and laughing about our trip home, and the fact that we were now the 'parents of six little short-legged, long-eared Beagle puppies.' They were quite a picture together. Suddenly we began to hear the puppies whining and barking. And the barking sounded like it was very close to our backdoor. Hubert got up to go see about them, came running back into the house and said, "Jo Ann, some are missing!. Get up and help me find them." The back of our yard was a little slope down to a narrow creek bed. There was a lot of undergrowth and we were so afraid they had wandered into the brush.

Again we started rounding them up, putting them back into the fenced in dog pen. As we counted, there were still two missing. Now it was beginning to get dark, and I saw the anxiety building in Hubert. I rounded up some of the kids in the neighborhood, who had not had a chance to even see the puppies yet, but we gathered a crowd and started walking the streets and yards. As of yet the dogs didn't have names. On our drive home I had pretty much named them all, only to have Hubert tell me that he could not picture him, and my Dad in the woods with a group of adult hunters calling, "here Punkin, here Precious, here Booty (that one had four white feet). So, here we were running up and down the streets calling, here Puppy, here Puppy! No dog is named just "Puppy." And, they never responded to that name.

I knew one thing about my husband, he always had a big heart for his hunting dogs . . . so I knew he would not give up until he found the last two. Now I was getting tired at this point so I said I was going back home, get some food and put it outside the door for the doggies in case they wondered back home. We lived in a hilly area but, I also knew that those little short-legged pups could really move it when they wanted to. As I was walking up the driveway, I saw the sweetest sight. It was truly a 'Kodak moment'. Both of the run-a-ways were laying down beside the front door. They had only been at their new home less than 24 hours and they found their way back home. Hallelujah! I began hollering loud enough for everyone to hear. This little 'search-party' experience turned out to be a fun time for our neighbors. As I've always heard said, 'if you want to meet people, get a dog'. Soon these six puppies became personal pets to all the neighbors. Then the day came when Hubert loaded them up and took them to my Dad for training. It was a very sad day. The only time I would see them is when we visited my parents.

Dad worked with the dogs in the woods getting them ready for hunting season. Daddy was the happiest I'd seen him in a long time. Then something began to happen with the dogs. They contracted the red mange that spread through the whole litter. Both Hubert and my Dad spent so much time, and money trying to cure them of this. The vets had done everything they knew to rid the dogs of this red mange. Only two of the dogs survived a year longer. The other four had to be put to sleep. What a sad time. Daddy didn't show his emotions very often, but I saw the biggest tears fall from that man's eyes. He always felt he should have been able to do more for them. The brief time they were part of our two families, they truly were a fun bunch. I'm not positive they would have ever passed the test of "true hunting dogs" . . . Dad had made them such pets he could not get a foot from them. They rode in the back of his truck to the store, and the bank. I could never visualize them in the brambles hunting rabbits. They couldn't get that far away from their treats Dad provided them. Eventually the two survivors succumbed to the same disease the other four had.

Dad and Hubert had such fun sharing their fish and hunting stories. Most of them were embellished beyond recognition.

CHAPTER 14

THE HOUSE HUBERT and I were building was completed in the spring of 1966. We moved in the first of April. Daddy died in October 1967 at the age of 63. It was the first time I had lost a close family member that I could remember. This was devastating for me. Daddy had survived his time in service, came home with such an illness to overcome, and now he had reached the point in his life that he could begin to enjoy some leisure time. He was admitted to the hospital in Columbia suffering from kidney problems. While he was recuperating from the kidney problem, he suffered a heart attack. He had spent 13 weeks in the hospital with these two illnesses. On the day he was to go home, he died in his sleep. It was determined from an autopsy, that he died of a pulmonary embolism. Mom was only 53 years old at the time.

At the time of my Dad's death, Mother had come to Columbia and was staying with Hubert and I while Dad was in the hospital for the 13 weeks before he died. She had gone home the Saturday before he was to be released from the hospital on Monday morning. She wanted to clean the house and yard, and then she grocery shopped and spent Sunday morning cooking all his favorite foods and desserts. She was so excited to be taking him back to the lake on Monday morning. At 2:00 a.m. Monday morning, the hospital called to say they had found him dead in his sleep.

When Mom and Dad married, she was 15 years old. Daddy used to tease her and say that he married her young so he could train her right. Their marriage was an example to my brothers and me of what a real 'love affair' was between a married couple. I'm sure they must have had arguments, but it surely took place behind closed doors, or out of the sound of their children. They laughed together. They prayed together and they showed the utmost respect for each other. As strong a person as she had always been for everyone else, Dad's sudden death was devastating for Mother.

My brothers and I had to go down to their lake house and dispose of all the food she had prepared for his homecoming from the long hospital stay. Mom continued to stay in Columbia with Hubert and I, trying to decide what she wanted to do with her life, now as a young widow. Mom was so young when they married, and she had never worked outside the home. Dad always took care of paying the bills, making major purchases, so Mother did not even know how to write a check, or balance a bank account, and knew nothing of the business world. Looking back now, I'm sure this is why she was always so positive and happy. Her world had revolved around Daddy. Her responsibility was taking care of her home and family. He had managed the finances.

During the year she stayed with us, I worked with her on the business and finances so she could survive on her own. I worked with her to close Dad's estate. Everything was transferred into her name. It was her decision to go back to the lake and live in the house Dad had literally built with his hands, a place where she had adjusted to call home. She had developed friendships within the church and community, and loved the place where she and Dad had enjoyed several years of their love for fishing. My brothers and I tried to let us tear down the cabin and build her a larger, more up-dated and comfortable house. She would not hear of this. This house was where she had found her happiness and she had learned to become quite independent in taking care of her business. She would usually ask the advice of her children, but we always knew that she had already made her decisions on most matters. This made us so proud of her.

Mom went home, took up her life and became quite a contributor to her church and community. She took on the responsibility of taking care of many seniors in the church and community. Taking them to doctor's appointments, grocery shopping and making sure they had their needs met. This was a quality Mother had instilled in me from a very early age when she took me with her to the 'Old Folks Home' to hand out hymn books and refreshments. Mom only finished the third grade in school. But, she could read and write. Her handwriting was much better than some college graduates who would send me notes. Her spelling was not always correct, but when she wrote that she and Daddy had been 'fishin' yesterday, there was no question where they had gone. Her lack of formal education did not keep her from sending greeting cards. Birthday, Get Well, Sympathy, Thinking of You. The red flag on our mailbox when I was a child was always up with cards addressed to both our family and friends, and anyone she thought needed to be cheered up. She bought cards by the boxes and was a regular customer at the post office for stamps. This was part of her ministry. She always said, "with my lack of education, there isn't a lot I can do, but I can send people a card to let them know I care." To this day, my red flag is up almost every day on my mailbox. If the postal department decides to lay off 120,000 workers and discontinue route mailmen, as they are predicting, I would be very unhappy. I have not learned on my PC to send the special occasion cards that are available. Somehow it takes away the enjoyment of being able to browse through the cards at the stores and read all the personal messages.

Chapter 15

H UBERT AND I were not blessed with children of our own, but we were blessed with a great niece and nephew of mine who were living in Columbia at the time. Misty was the cutest little red headed, freckled faced girl in the world. She had such a pleasant, infectious personality and became the apple of my eye when she was born. We would keep her at times for her parents and there was no question, she was our surrogate child. When she was four years old we took her to Disney World in Orlando. Then four years later, her little brother Adam came into the world. When Misty was eight and Adam four years old, we made our second trip to Disney World, Sea World and the Kennedy Space Center. Adam was Hubert's little buddy. They spent many weekends with us. I loved taking them shopping for clothes. They traveled with us and were such fun to have around. Their parents moved back to Florence, SC and Hubert and I were saddened greatly at this. Many Friday afternoons Hubert would take off work early to drive to Florence and pick the kids up from school and bring them to Columbia for the weekends.

On Saturdays, Hubert and Adam would go fishing at the river, catch big turtles to carry home in a bucket of water. Misty and I would go shopping and have lunch. Adam used to say, "Aunt Jo, Uncle Hubert and I are going to go to our hide-out, you and Misty go do *gurl* stuff." And that's exactly what we did. We took them to the Zoo, the Circus, Town Theatre for plays, we had picnics in the parks. They were our kids and we loved them as our own.

It was such fun for me to take Misty shopping. I had always dreamed that one day I would have a little girl to dress in 'frills and bows', and I would have a little red headed freckled faced boy. Somehow the plans got screwed up. She came with the red hair and freckles, he came with blond hair and clear fair skin. She did not like frills and bows, and he was the typical boy who loved to fish and play with insects and animals. The years spent with Misty and Adam were some of the happiest years of our marriage. During their high school years we didn't get to see them as often because they developed their own friends and interests.

CHAPTER 16

"A Year of Change"

H UBERT WORKED WITH Southern Bell Telephone
Company from the time he graduated from high
school. He was very happy with the Company and enjoyed
every day of his working for them. In 1982, AT& T became
the "mother" of the Bell Companies. This was the year of the
divestiture of Southern Bell. During this process, the company
had offered some management employees an option package of
early retirement, benefits for which he qualified. At the young
age of 51, Hubert took this early retirement package. It was
probably the worst thing he could have done, considering that
he had worked all his life, was such an active person with energy
of a teenager, and anxiety to go along with it. Hubert was very
intelligent, loved to read and expand his mind. He was curious
about anything he did not understand or know, and he had so
many hobbies and interests. Fortunately at this time, money
was not an issue with either of us. He had every reason to be

contented with his decision to retire early so he could enjoy his hobbies. Time would prove otherwise.

Over the next few years, we continued to travel, but I noticed that his interests had waned on almost every area of his life. Looking back over the years now, I realize that Hubert went through some sad times that I should have recognized as depression. It is an illness that finds a way to hide itself until it erupts into a serious physical and mental condition.

1982 was the same year my younger brother, David was diagnosed with lung cancer that had mastisized to the brain. He was still working at his shop, and still repairing automobiles. Ricky, his younger son had been working with him learning the trade. On a Sunday morning, Mother called me from the lake and said that I needed to check on David. Usually he went down to visit Mother almost every weekend he was in town. She had not seen, nor heard from him in over two weeks, and she just thought he may be out-of-town. She had called him earlier that morning to see how he was doing. Her conversation with him was very alarming for Mom. She said he was talking like he may have had a stroke, with slurred words and confusion, not making sense when she questioned him.

I was getting ready for church when Mother called me. This concerned me as well, so I called David myself. Like Mother had said, he wasn't making much sense in his conversation, but he said, "Sis, I'm doing fine, don't worry." The feeling in my stomach told me that indeed there was something wrong with him. Instead of going to church that morning, I drove across town to David's house. As soon as he opened the door I could see that he had a problem. His eyes were bloodshot and watery and he was still in his pajamas. He was always an early riser and the time was around 10:30 in the morning.

He was sitting in his lounge chair in the den, and he had a cigarette burning in the ashtray. David was a very neat, articulate housekeeper. He had been divorced quite a few years and lived alone, but he always kept a very nice house. When I looked in his kitchen, what I saw was enough to convince me that he definitely had a problem. There were dishes in the sink, on the table, and a frying pan and pots on the stove, with food still in them.

I sat down with him in the den and began to observe his actions. I immediately noticed that he continued dropping his cigarette on the floor. This was scary because of catching the carpet on fire. He was trying to hold the cigarette in his right hand but I could see that he had no control over his hand and arm. I put the cigarette out when it fell to the floor, and asked him if he had been feeling bad recently. He said. "No, Sis, I'm fine." I happened to see on the coffee table a packet of Valium tablets and asked him when he had started taking this. He then told me that a doctor at the emergency room at one of our hospitals had given it to him. He had realized one night that something didn't seem right and went to the emergency room. Apparently the exam they gave him wasn't very extensive because they sent him away with a packet of Valium. Later, I thought that there was a chance he could not describe his problem to the medics, because he was having difficulty describing it to me.

David had been very healthy as a child, and he had not been sick as he got older. He did not drink alcohol, other than an occasional beer. He could not stand the smell of alcohol. I was at a loss in what was going on with him, but I knew that there was definitely something not right with his present condition. I knew David's family doctor, so I asked him if I could come take him to see the doctor on Monday. Just for a check-up. He agreed that he would go see Dr. Clark, but he could drive himself. He *promised* me he would go and call me with the diagnosis. I knew he would keep his promise to go, so I asked him if he wanted me to stay with him the rest of the day and night. I was concerned about his smoking. He then promised me that he would not smoke after I left, he even was agreeable to giving me his smoking materials.

Monday I had him on my mind all day. Sure enough, late that afternoon David called to say that Dr. Clark said he could not find anything wrong with him. Still, I did not feel convinced of this. David went to the shop on Tuesday and again on Wednesday. On Wednesday afternoon, Michael, his older son called and was so concerned about his dad. David had reached the point that he could not sign checks with his right hand and was beginning to slur his words much more. I asked Mike to pick up some chicken that evening, and he and Ricky meet me at David's house. I called

David and told him that we were having 'dinner' at his house and we were bringing the food. He was delighted.

We all arrived around 5:30 on Wednesday afternoon. David had set the dining room table, had poured our glasses with Pepsi, and was looking forward to our coming. We had casual conversation for a few minutes. Then we noticed that he could not hold his piece of chicken, and he spilled his glass of Pepsi on the table. This is when we were truly convinced that we had to get him help. Ricky spent the night with him. The next morning I made a trip to Dr. Clark's office. After discussing both David's visit on Monday, and what we had been seeing in him, Dr. Clark said, "I knew Dave was not being honest with me when I saw him on Monday. He kept saying he was just tired and would not tell me any symptoms he was having." Immediately Dr. Clark said, "you need to bring him back into my office this afternoon and I will get him to the hospital so we can begin running some tests. There's something seriously wrong with Dave and I know now exactly where to begin testing." We did get David to the doctor that day. His doctor sent him directly to the hospital and they ran tests. The tests showed numerous tumors in both lungs. They were sure it was cancer. It was so progressed that the same day they did an MRI and found it had gone to the brain, with multiple tumors there as well. This explained all the obvious symptoms he was having.

When I arrived at the hospital that afternoon, I met the pulmonary doctor coming from his room. He stopped me with the diagnosis report. This was devastating news for me. David and I had been so close growing up. Even though he had been a *'mean brother'* to me growing up, playing tricks on me, and we could fight like cats and dogs at times, he was still my *best* buddy and I loved him dearly.

Immediately we had him moved to a hospital that was more specialized in cancer. He stayed there for seven days before the doctors told us that there was absolutely nothing they could do but keep him comfortable. The doctor had said he had less than one month to live. He had already begun to lose use of his limbs, and was mumbling his words. There was a real nice nursing home only a mile from my house. I made the arrangements to have him moved there so I could be with him more. Mother came to Columbia and stayed with me so she could be with him during the daytime. Hubert or I would stay with him at night.

Hubert and David had grown up together, been best friends. They had fished together, attended automobile races, and played ball together. Hubert always considered David his brother rather than brother-in-law.

From the day of David's diagnosis of cancer until his death it was 30 days. David was 49 years old when he died. His cancer was most surely derived from his smoking habit since he was fourteen years old. He was too young to die. Like all of David's family, Hubert was there for him every day. He was so saddened by David's sudden illness and death that it only deepened his problem of depression. It was like losing his own brother.

David had been divorced for several years. He now owned the automobile body shop where he had grown up working alongside my Dad since his graduation from high school. Cars had always been a great interest and he was as gifted as my Dad was in the repair of automobiles. When he died, his two young boys, Mike and Ricky were devastated. His younger son, Ricky had been working at the shop with him. His older son, Michael had pursued other interests.

Before David died, he had lost use of his body and could not speak. We knew he could hear us because of the expressions he made with his eyes as he tried to respond to conversations. We never had a chance to discuss his wishes or funeral plans. I could not have that conversation with him. I could take care of those when the time came.

There is one *precious memory* I will cherish the rest of my life. One that we experienced while he was in the cancer hospital before we moved him to the nursing home. When we were growing up, we loved to listen to the 'Lone Ranger' on the radio each afternoon at 4:00. He would take his paper route early so he would be home for this program. I belonged to the Lone Ranger Club, had my badge to prove it. We would sit together in a big armchair in the living room, right beside the table that held the radio. Mom would fix us some popcorn occasionally and we'd have our Pepsi Cola. This was like a ritual every day for us.

One afternoon when I was on my way to visit David in the hospital, I stopped by Cromer's Peanuts and bought a big bag of freshly popped corn. When I got to the hospital, one of the nurses saw me and I explained to her what we used to do as kids as we listened to the 'Lone Ranger'. Shortly after I went into David's room, the nurse came in with two big cups of ice and a bottle of Pepsi. You should have seen David's eyes. I crawled up on the bed, we had our little afternoon party . . . unfortunately, we couldn't listen to the 'Lone Ranger' anymore. He could still swallow his food at this point and we ate half of that big bag of popcorn. He just smiled and winked at me the whole time we were eating.

After David's death, his attorney called to tell me that he was in possession of David's will and that he would like to meet with me and his two sons for the reading of the will.

Through the years David and I had been very close, however we had never discussed his personal, nor his business affairs. He had not told me that he had named me as Executrix of his Estate. At the reading of the will, it appeared to be a rather simple will. He had named his sons as the beneficiaries of his Estate. This should have been pretty simple to execute, but he had a business that his young son had been trying to run while he was in the hospital and nursing center before his death. Needless to say, I was almost without a sense of direction as to where to start with taking care of his estate and the business at this point.

Because his boys were entirely too young, and inexperienced in the business world to continue operating the shop, I had to spend the next year virtually reconstructing his business, and his personal affairs before I could begin to probate his will. There were insurance policies and deeds that had to be checked out, and property disposed of. My dining room was turned into an office. During this time, I incorporated the business in an effort to give some protection for his sons as they continued to do some work at the shop. The shop had always been operated as a proprietorship. I tried to help them make the right decision of what was best for them. This was especially difficult for Ricky because he was realizing that D & D Body Works, as it had been operating in the Columbia area since 1943, and under the ownership of the Doub family, would no longer exist. The building located at 928 Washington Street was years later, put on the Historic Registry of Buildings unique in architectural facades. It was purchased and renovated inside into a beautiful single level office building. The name D & D Body Works, which was painted in white, is still visible on the building. I stopped by one day and the secretary was kind enough to give me a tour of the building. It was unbelievable. It may just be an old building to the owners, but I could stand in the conference room and remember all the summers I worked on an old dented car fender out back of Dad's shop. It was such a *precious memory.* I got back in my car and drove home, with tears running down my face. I'm so grateful that the building still stands.

To begin the process of executing David's Estate, I literally brought every file and piece of paper related to the business to my house, as well as going through his house and collecting his personal checks, insurance documents, and other information that could help in this task. I went through each transaction in his files, one by one.

CHAPTER 17

ALL OF THE events that were transpiring created sad times for Hubert. It was during this period that he decided we should take his *dream trip* to Australia "What, I exclaimed! Surely you are joking with me." But, he was adamant about making the trip. There could not have been a more inconvenient time in our lives for us to plan a three week trip so far away from home. I even entertained the thought that perhaps he was so depressed with David's death, and the fact that I was spending every minute at home sitting around my dining room table trying to reconstruct David's business and personal affairs, that he just wanted to get away from the sad events that had taken place. And for me, I had taken so much time away from work during David's illness, and planning his funeral, that I was reluctant to request an additional three weeks for a vacation trip.

We had made friends with a couple from Sidney, Australia on one of our trips out West. They had continued to correspond with us through the years and had offered many invitations for us to come to Australia for a visit. The reason we had not taken this trip earlier was because of Hubert's fear of flying. Each time we had flown to Europe for vacations, it was not a pleasant trip. Remembering these times, I was not interested in sitting next to him on a plane for the long flight. It always brought fear to me that Hubert could become so ill from depression and anxiety that he would have to be hospitalized in a foreign country. But, it seemed that Hubert was determined to make plans for this trip. I began to feel that the stress of what had transpired with his early retirement, David's death, and my spending my time working on the monumental task of his estate, had made him think that things would all work out just fine if we left the country for a while. In fact, I felt that Hubert was actually running away from his problems.

After discussing my situation with my boss, and being granted the three weeks time off for our trip, Hubert began making the necessary plans. Wiring our friends in Sidney for their approval of the time we would be arriving, making our airline reservations and getting all our documents necessary for the trip The plans were in place. Everything was working out for our trip. I began to notice that Hubert was getting excited about making the trip, or at least I was interpreting his efforts organizing everything, as excitement. But, one day at the office I received a phone call from Hubert's doctor. He told me that he had Hubert in his office and he was in a very bad state of anxiety. So much so, that he wanted me to come get him and take him to the Baptist Hospital where he had made arrangements for him to be admitted for treatment and observation. We were only two weeks away from our departure to Australia when our situation changed again. It was brought to a climax when Hubert began to realize how long we would be flying. His fear of flying had overtaken his desire to enjoy his dream vacation. Even in 1982, travel to Australia was expensive. For some reason, I had asked him to take out travel insurance on the cost of the trip. Thankfully he had followed my advice, so when we cancelled our trip because of his ending up in the hospital, we were able to re-coup a portion of our expenses. It did cost us $1,200 that was not refunded.

For the next few years, things were up and down as many changes were occurring in our lives. There were some very happy days of traveling, spending time in the mountains, beaches, having fish fry cook outs for our friends and neighbors. It was evident that the one thing that my husband did not handle well was any major change in his life that disrupted his normal routine. If it was a change at work, home or within the family, it was as if he could not control the situation and it touched off his feeling depressed and becoming very anxious. When we built our first house, he did not want to move into it . . . he didn't like having to re-establish the lawn. Everything was supposed to be perfect, and he did everything possible to make things perfect. He was obsessive about things being exactly as he envisioned them to be.

Through the years, we had talked about buying a little cabin in the mountains because we both loved the area around Blowing

Rock, N.C. We enjoyed the cooler weather, and he could just visualize fishing in a mountain stream. So, In 1990, we finally found a lot in Blowing Rock and purchased it to build a house where we could spend summer vacations and holidays, because I was still working. In the summer of 1991 we began building our home there. It was exciting because he had taken such an interest in choosing just the right location, and even looked into working as a forest ranger there on the Blue Ridge Parkway. We had spent many weeks during the summer in Blowing Rock choosing building materials and buying furniture for the house. It was going to be a great time in our lives now that he had begun to deal with his depression. My prayers seemed to be working, because since the time Hubert began with depression, I had prayed that God would provide the peace and contentment he needed to help him overcome his mental illness and find new life in his retirement years.

CHAPTER 18

A T THE SAME time we were beginning this new phase of our lives, I had enrolled in night school and was attending class three nights a week. I was working full time, studying every night that I was not in school and making all the plans for our new house in the mountains, including drawing the plans for the house. Things were pretty busy and I thought, on the right tract again. But, as the building began, the stress of change brought about the depression again for Hubert. This time it was the worst ever. He would sit at home and worry about the builder in North Carolina and whether they were doing a good job. I could not get him to go up and be there during the early building process. Even though the builder we hired was one of the best in Blowing Rock, and he was making a video of the building process from the clearing of the lot until we were to move into the house. The excitement of our fulfilling another of our dreams was over-shadowed by his worry, anxiety and deep depression.

Soon Hubert would not leave the house, he would not take his clothes off to sleep at night. He would just sit in a chair all night, or walk the floor. Ultimately he would end up in one of the hospitals psychiatric floors under heavy medication, or he would be in a private institution for a period of 30 days. This time it was the most severe case of depression that some of his doctors had dealt with. There were two occasions when he tried to take his life, and he would again have to be hospitalized until we felt he no longer had those thoughts. He lost his desire and excitement for the house in the mountains, and refused to take any responsibility or interest in it. I took over this project.

I would leave our home in West Columbia at 4:00 in the morning, drive 200 miles to Blowing Rock, meet with the builder and go pick out materials necessary for completing the house, drive home to Columbia and go to school for three hours, then study the rest of the night for an exam the next evening. I would get up at 5:00 the next morning to study, go by the hospital to see Hubert and then to work, and back to school that evening. This was our life's existence for over six months.

During the period of building, I would make trips to the mountains, take things for the house and leave them in the basement of our house. In January of 1992 the house was completed. Hubert would not go with me to see it, so I made the trip to have furniture delivered on one of the coldest and windy days they had on record. It was raining, sleeting, and winds blowing in gusts of 65 miles per hour. Traveling alone in this weather on mountain roads certainly increased my 'prayer life'.

Through all the times I had to handle emergency situations with my husband, it was my faith in God that gave me both physical and mental strength to get through each one. I knew that God was my rock to lean on during these nightmares we were experiencing, and I believed His promise that He would not give me any burden that was more than I could handle, *if* I would just trust Him.

On January 4, 1992, I moved into our house on Misty Mountain, Blowing Rock, N.C. The house had one of the most beautiful scenic views of Grandfather Mountain. You could witness the sunrises and sunsets from the porches and decks. It was an awesome view. The furniture store delivered all of our new furniture and helped me set everything up. My builder, Nick Lyons and his wife, Robbie had cleaned the house and washed all the windows. The business relationship with our builder and his family had become a real friendship during the year he was building our house. I could not have completed the house without their support.

It was in late February after the house was completed before Hubert would see it in its completion. He could not believe how everything had turned out. I thought that he showed some interest, and a bit of excitement in getting up there to begin landscaping the yard. Of course, in February at 4,000 feet in the mountains, there's not much landscaping that can be done. So by the time spring and summer came, again it was a time that he was deep into his depression. He had begun to worry about not being able to finish the yards with the landscaping until summertime. The anxiety started building and the depression had again taken over his thoughts and ability to function. He was heavily medicated to the point that walking to the mailbox each day seemed quite a chore. And driving was prohibited because of the medication. So with his being confined and my working, there was entirely too much time for him to spend thinking about his not being able to deal with his illness.

Again, I was to realize that life comes at you full force at times and you wonder how you will be able to deal with the situations and survive with any semblance of a sane mind. But, during the summer of '92 Hubert did make two other trips to the house in the mountains. In September he went with Mom and I for a weekend. We had invited my Mother's sister, Anna Mae, and her daughter, Betty Kay from Winston-Salem to spend the weekend with us.

Since Hubert's birthday was on the 18th of September and my cousin, Betty Kay's was on the 29th, we celebrated both birthdays over the weekend. Actually we enjoyed a nice weekend together, other than Hubert's being very quiet and staying to himself. I noticed he did not want to go outside. He was concerned that the yard was not finished and he could not work in it because of being so medicated. Of course during these periods he was heavily medicated, he did not drive a car.

When we got home to Columbia on Sunday evening, Hubert told my Mother that he would be taking her home to Santee on Monday morning. This seemed a bit strange because Hubert always enjoyed having Mother visit. During the periods of his severe depression and not being able to drive, Mother would drive to Columbia to pick him up and take him to spend several days with her at the lake. They had a relationship that was more a 'mother-son' love. She would cook all his favorite foods and drive him wherever he wanted to go. Mother was a person who could talk the horns off a 'billy goat' when she wanted to, but she was also the most wonderful person you could ever turn to for listening to your problems. She was such a help to me during these months while I was trying to work. Hubert loved spending time with Mom.

Monday morning I left for work and Hubert got up and showered and was helping Mother pact to go home. When I got home from work on Monday evening, I prepared dinner and we talked about our house in the mountains. I thought that he would begin to realize how much he could enjoy our new home there.

On Tuesday afternoon when I arrived home from work, I found a note on the desk that he had gone to Charleston for a few days. I did not hear from him on Tuesday night nor on

Wednesday. He had left home on several occasions during times when he wanted to work out his problems. Some times he would be gone for several days before I heard from him. These times were so stressful for me because some times he would not let me know where he was, and would not call me. If you've ever had a loved one out of your contact, especially when you know they are depressed, you can understand how my worry would keep me up all night.

Thursday nights were my weekly appointment at the beauty shop and I would go directly from work. When I arrived home, Hubert was still not home and there were no phone messages from him. I started doing laundry and cleaning house. I did not prepare dinner because I didn't know when he would be coming home. Or if he would be coming home.

At around 6:30 that evening my doorbell rang. When I opened the door, there stood his sister and her husband, and Hubert's brother and his wife. I thought they had just come for a visit, but then they told me the news that Hubert had taken his life that morning in a motel room in Orangeburg, S. C. He was found by the motel cleaning lady later in the day. He had left a note for me. The day was Thursday, October 1, 1992. There will never be a day in my life that my heart will break as it did at hearing this news. This will forever be the *darkest* day of my life.

Although there had been nights I had sat up all night talking to God and trying to "fix Hubert's problem." Two weeks before this tragedy happened, I had knelt beside my bed, sobbing tears that would fill a bathtub, as I finally committed Hubert to God for the healing of his mind from this depression that was literally destroying his life. After getting up from this long, soul-wrenching time with God, I had actually felt a peace and calm come over me. That night I took a bath, and for the first time in months, went to bed and fell asleep immediately. I now realize that for so many weeks, months, and years, I had sought the best doctors and specialists, the best hospitals that were available at the time to try to help Hubert. But, I could not FIX him.

There's just something about losing a loved one at their own hand that causes you to begin to wonder. During the years Hubert suffered with his depression and anxiety, did I do enough to prevent this from happening? Was I as understanding as I should have been with his illness? Was it all my fault? Why did God not answer my prayers and heal Hubert from this horrible illness? Was life with me so terrible that I was the cause of him taking his own life? Was he so unhappy with the fact that he thought he had made a big mistake by retiring too early? I could go on and on with questions about what had happened to Hubert.

In the eyes of his family and friends, he had all the reasons in the world to be happy and content with his life. Until this very day, I deal with these, and numerous other questions.

As in every event that happens in our lives, there is always some lesson we learn from it. In the tragedy that happened in the lives of our family in losing Hubert, I feel that I have learned to recognize depression as a disease that has to be dealt with early. It is one that you have to feel compassion for the people who suffer from mental illness, as well as the love ones who see the effects of depression and how it destroys individuals. I still do not understand the illness. I have learned that, although the medical profession has come a long way towards treating depression, there is absolutely nothing that anyone, other than the person who experiences depression, can do to change this illness. It is an illness of the mind, and it is one of the mysteries of mankind. It is also alarming to read the statistics of people who suffer from this very debilitating illness, and like cancer, it is no respecter of age. Many people today who suffer from depression still view this illness as one that is shameful and keep it to themselves until it becomes too far advanced to treat.

The one fact that always concerned me in the treatment of this illness, is that there is entirely too much addictive medication given to patients in hospitals for treatment of depression and anxiety that effects the mind, and body in a negative way. There was never a time during my husband's illness and treatment that I didn't feel he was over-medicated. At times he could not function. At one time during his treatment, he was on six addictive drugs. The drugs were mind-altering that took away his ability to think and reason. There were days at home that he could not walk to the mailbox to get the mail. I realize that the treatment for depression has changed. In early years I knew that they actually locked people up in the asylum, strapped them to their beds after receiving electro-shock treatments. During Hubert's treatment, I thought about this. And, there were times when he was so sedated that he was, in my mind, experiencing the same treatment. For he was being held in a dysfunctional state under the influence of psychotic drugs.

As a kid growing up, Mother had a little prayer plaque hanging over her stove in the kitchen. It read:

> '***Lord, help me to remember—***
> ***There is nothing going to happen to me today,***
> ***That You and I together can't handle . . .***'

Mother believed it then, . . . and ***I*** believe it today . . . !

Through it all, God gave me the courage and strength to provide the medical help available for my husband. I was blessed to work for a company who understood what I was going through and allowed me to take care of Hubert's needs as they came up, even when I had to leave my office in a moment's notice, and sometimes did not come back for days. It is only through my strong faith in God that I was able to be a caregiver during these very dark days. I began putting my life back together and with the help of God, my family, and the understanding support of my friends, I live each day, still with sadness at the helplessness I saw in my husband as he dealt with his demons of depression.

CHAPTER 19

DURING THE YEAR following Hubert's death, things began to fall back into place for me at work. The transition and adjustments I had to make at this time were a bit over-whelming. I was taking care of our home in West Columbia, our mountain home in Blowing Rock, N. C., as well as taking care of my Mother who still lived at Santee on the lake. There wasn't a lot of time for me to have a 'pity-party'. It was by having such strong friends surrounding me that I was able to cope with the feeling of "oneness" that exists after losing a spouse who had been *my* support and care-giver. But, God kept His promise again. He did not allow anything to come into my life that He and I together could not handle. Although I have to be absolutely honest, there were times when I wondered if some events could have been spaced a little farther apart.

Six Months Later . . .

It was the 25th of March, 1993, that I received a call from my brother Robert, that Mother had fallen at the lake and someone had found her at her boat ramp. They had taken her to the hospital in Orangeburg where they had found she had broken her hip. Immediately I was at the hospital when they determined that surgery would be necessary the next day. Mother was 79 years old at the time. She had spent the years after my Dad's death living at the lake by herself, and had become quite independent. Although she had lost her husband, her son, and a son-in-law that she treasured as her own son, she had still been a true source of encouragement for me. We had a wonderful mother-daughter relationship, even though she always believed that I was truly a "Daddy's Girl."

Mother came through the hip replacement surgery fine. I stayed with her at night and my brother and sister-in-law would come early in the morning to stay during the day. I was still working in Columbia and would drive to Orangeburg after work to spend the nights with her. The night duty was a real trip. Mother began having hallucinations during the night time. She saw ballerinas dancing out of the sink. There were soldiers surrounding the house, (that was where she thought she was), and then there were bugs crawling all over the ceiling. Now, I had taken care of family members in the hospital before, but this was a real scary experience. After the nurses convinced me that it was the pain medication that was causing these strange little episodes,

I had to humor Mom by hanging a towel over the sink so she couldn't see the ballerinas dancing. I had to go talk to the soldiers that were surrounding the house, and then I got a newspaper and began killing the bugs on the ceiling. Only one problem, I couldn't kill the darn bugs fast enough . . . she kept seeing them move all around the room. It was truly a HOOT! If her doctor had walked in to see me in my stocking feet, standing on a chair in the middle of the room, with a newspaper rolled up swinging at non-existent bugs, I'm sure I would have been hauled off to the psychiatric ward in the hospital. Not to be making light of Mom's condition, or state of mind from the medicine, but it did make the nights pass faster for me. As I would be driving back to Columbia in the mornings, thinking about the night we had experienced, I could not help but laugh out loud. Of course by the time my brother arrived at the hospital to relieve me in the mornings, Mom had slept off the drugs, and was the dear sweet Mother, who never believed me when I related my 'nightmare' of the previous evening's event. (Night duty nurses should receive 'combat pay')

After a week in the Orangeburg Hospital, Mother was transferred to Health South in Columbia for rehab treatment. She continued to experience some confusion about things, but her doctors said she would be fine as soon as the anesthesia got out of her body. They said that older people experienced some confusion as a result of anesthesia during surgery.

When she arrived in Columbia, I mentioned this confusion to the doctor who was going to be treating her. He agreed to keep watch of this and determine if there could be another problem. After a week and a half, I received a call that they would like permission to have an MRI done on Mother. As a result, they determined that she had a tumor on her brain the size of a lemon that was putting pressure on her brain and could cause her to lose her eyesight if not taken care of. WOW! This was not good news. It was a decision that Robert and I faced, as well as Mother, to determine if she could survive the surgery after only going through hip replacement within less than two weeks. After discussing the options with her doctors, we decided to first present the facts to Mom and see if she could make the decision for surgery. When the doctor went with us to give her the news, and her options, he said, "Miss Jessie, you have something that is in your head pressing on your brain. If we don't do something about this, you could lose your eyesight." We had told the doctor that if she could not make a decision, we would then determine what was best for her. Well, she just looked up at the doctor, after pondering for a few minutes and said, "Well Doc, I surely don't want to lose my eyes, so you just go in there and take that thing out of my brain." Within a day, she was scheduled for surgery which lasted 6 ½ hours. The surgery was successful, the tumor was not cancer, and the only thing affected was her short-term memory. Within a two week period, this little 79 year old lady had gone through a hip replacement and a 6 ½ hour brain surgery. I'd say she was *one tough cookie*!

As a result of the two surgeries, her doctors recommended that she go to an assisted living facility for a period until we could determine just how much loss of memory she would have, and whether she could live by herself at the lake. On May 15, 1993, Mother's Day, she was transferred to a facility close to me. It was close enough that I could visit her 3 or 4 times a week. This was more than I saw her when she lived at Santee so she was very happy.

Again, my situation was going to change. It seemed my life took a different direction quite frequently now. I was back at work, keeping up three houses and yards now that Mother was in the assisted living facility. One house was 200 miles away in the mountains of NC, one 80 miles away at Santee, SC, and my home in West Columbia, SC. And again . . . through all this added responsibility, God was good. Things had all worked out and I was managing pretty well, or at least I *thought* I was.

On Labor Day 1993, I had invited some friends to spend the holiday weekend with me in the mountains. While I was there I remember experiencing some shortness of breath when we walked around the mountain, but I did not feel sick. I came home and went back to work. On September 9th, I suddenly got sick. Seriously ill with fever of 102-104 degrees. I was hospitalized with double pneumonia. I spent the next 20 days in the hospital while the doctors tried to determine where the infection had come from. I was tested for Rocky Mountain Tick Fever because of my symptoms and having spent time in the mountains. Rocky

Mountain Tick Fever was ruled out. The source of the infection was not determined and I was released two days after my fever finally broke on the 18th day being in the hospital. The doctors told me that I would have to be off work for a month and a half.

Fortunately for me I guess, my doctor had been through the many emergencies and crises that faced my husband and I during his times with depression. He knew we had this house in the mountains. His prescription for me when I left the hospital, along with three other medicines, was that I go to the house in the mountains for my recuperating period.

After Hubert's death, I considered selling our house in the mountains. I prayed for God's guidance in making a rational decision regarding our mountain home. Somehow the house and location seemed to be my source of healing and strength from a very long period of time dealing with the stress of Hubert's illness. It was as if this was a part of God's plan to provide this source of peace for me. I rested at home for a few days and then packed up and made the trip to the mountains. When I looked at myself in the full-length mirror in my bedroom, it was a scary sight. My eyes were set back in my head, my hair had begun to fall out due to the high fevers for so long, and I had lost over 15 pounds. I didn't like what I saw, and realized just how sick I had been.

It was in the fall of the year in Blowing Rock and one of the most beautiful and vivid color seasons I ever remember in the mountains. I spent the month of October and half of November in a healing process, both emotionally and physically. My friends would come up to spend time with me during my stay. Looking back over that period of my life, I believe that God was drawing a plan for my future and giving me the physical strength to deal with it. When I returned home, and back to work, life was beginning to take on some meaning again.

My questions were not all answered about what had taken place over the past few years, nor had I been able to understand why it was not in God's plan for Hubert to overcome his illness, as I had asked for in my prayers. But I came to realize that I would never have those answers while I was on earth. Through all this period, God was still my source of strength. The contraction of my pneumonia after the death of my husband, and the surgeries and relocation of mother had taken its toll on my physical body, to say nothing of the effect it had on my mind. But, through it all . . . I still had my faith and confidence that God had a plan for me. This was confirmed when I made my first follow-up visit to the doctors who told me that I had been one 'lucky lady' to have survived the severity of my illness. I knew it wasn't *LUCK* that had brought me through this ordeal. It was *God's* hand on my life. It was also the concern of two of my dear friends, Sandra and Bill Windham, who found me at home that Sunday with the high fever and took me to the emergency room.

These two precious friends didn't just leave me in the emergency room for treatment. They have continued to stay by me through the years of good times, and some not-so-good. In reading one of my little books given to me by my '*Magnolia*' girlfriend, Joyce Rabon, I could not help but think of Bill and Sandra.

> '*A friend is one who stands to share*
> *Your every touch of grief and care.*
> *He comes by chance, but stays by choice;*
> *Your praises he is quick to voice.*
> *No grievous fault or passing whim*
> *Can make an enemy of him.*
> *And though your need be great or small,*
> *His strength is yours through it all.*
> *No matter where your path may turn*
> *Your welfare is his chief concern.*
> *No Matter what your dream may be*
> *He prays your triumph soon to see . . .*'
> —Edgar A. Guest—

Friends are God's gift to us on earth to provide a source of love and encouragement . . . and God blessed me with His great generosity of friends in my life. Now there are *ACQUAINTANCES*, and then there are *FRIENDS*. There is a world of difference in the two. My group of friends, I honestly believe, would make many sacrifices for me if I needed them to, and they would do it without any thought of restitution or reward. I have an 'acquaintance' who is a lovely lady. She seemingly knows the most influential, and important people in our city and state as if they were her 'personal' friends. I call this "name dropping." Because if truth be known, she is about as 'acquainted' with these people as I am. And I have no more relationship, or knowledge of these people than what I hear on the TV or read in the newspaper. There have been times when I was tempted to say, "well, if I were you, I'd be a little more selective in choosing my *friends*." Now, there I go again . . . letting my mouth take over my better judgment. My point is, if this lady should have a real crisis or need in her life, I question how many of these '*special friends*' she could call on to give help, comfort and support to her.

'Better one true friend than a hundred acquaintances.'
-Early American Proverb-

'The MAGNOLIAS'

Shortly after my husband's death, a group of eight friends began going to the movies, out to dinner, attend theatre and concerts, and just share our circumstances. All of us had great jobs, were involved with church and family, but we seemed to have a common ground when is came to understanding each other's feelings. Our ages ranged from 50-54. Of this group, one was single, one divorced, and the other six were widows who had all lost their husbands within a year to eighteen months of one another. It was a wonderful support group and we began calling ourselves, "*The Magnolias*", partly because of the movie, '*STEEL MAGNOLIAS*'. This group of girls was certainly made of the strength of *steel* and the beauty of the *Magnolia*. We had all experienced great losses and had overcome our tragedies. Our group continues today with the same eight girls. (Actually, we're very *mature* girls). We have experienced deaths of children, grandchildren, parents, brothers and sisters, aunts and uncles, and have survived various personal illnesses and hardships. Through it all, we have kept our strong faith in God, our determination that we can continue with our lives and make a difference in our families, and indeed our community through the various ways we share our time and talents.

There are no dues, no rules, no requirements for our group. We have a Purpose, a Club Statement, and a Club Motto. We have never solicited new members. Not because we are prejudiced, selfish or "snooty" for lack of a better word; we simply have a common bond that we feel God placed us in a position at a time when we had strength that we could share with one another.

The purpose of 'The Magnolias' is to provide spiritual, emotional, and social support to its members, and to contribute to the quality of life for our fellowman.

CLUB STATEMENT

"Kind words indeed warm the human spirit. Kindness is literally love in action. Showing genuine friendship to others by regarding them as important in God's sight and worthy of dignity and respect. It involves treating others with courtesy, lending encouragement, and freely offering yourself or your resources to help a person in need, no strings attached . . ."

CLUB MOTTO

"When she speaks, her words are wise, and kindness is the rule for everything she says"
Proverbs 31:26

This simple purpose of our group was signed by eight of the greatest friends I have ever known:

Marceil Mangum	*Alsie Kelley*
Sylvia Powell	*Mary Jones*
Joyce Rabon	*Bertie Bryant*
Loretta (Frye) Steedly	*Jo Ann (Rogers) Broome*

Each year we use the calendar and assign each girl a specific month to be hostess. It is totally her responsibility to plan an activity for that month. We meet the 4th Thursday in each month at 6:30 pm. On our first official meeting our hostess had planned an Easter visit to our Children's Hospital Cancer Unit at one of our local hospitals. We carried gifts and treats for each child we visited. What a great time we had to see the smiles on the children's faces. We made trips to my mountain house, to the beach house of another member. We went bowling, picnics in the parks (by candlelight), attended concerts, plays, and movies. We have taken two and three day Christmas trips and one five day cruise to the Caribbean.

Some of my most precious, and funniest memories are of trips made to my mountain house. Now I'm not a shopper who enjoys having relatives or friends tag along when I'm shopping. Usually I'm on a mission, focused on exactly what I'm looking for and in a specific store. So when the eight of the 'Magnolias' would go shopping in Blowing Rock we would split up. We would decide how much time we needed to cover the stores, meet back at a central location at the specified time and then determine if we needed extra time. After completely covering each store, we would meet at our designated spot and plan our lunch, or dinner. Each girl would usually have numerous bags which we piled in the back of the two vehicles needed to transport us. That evening, after we had our dinner, we would have "Show and Tell." We would gather around in the living room with our individual bags of goodies and the rule was; Each girl would show what they had purchased. And, if it was an article of clothing, it was to be modeled.

On one such trip, one of the girls, Sylvia, had made quite a large purchase of nice lingerie from the Hanes Outlet Store.

I guess she was not thinking ahead of how this was going to play out in our "Show and Tell" that evening. After everyone had emptied their bags which contained everything from cooking ware to linens and bedding to paintings, a huge variety of items. Sylvia was the last to make her presentation. She opened her bag and showed us the nice lingerie she had purchased . . . only to have the group staring at her, waiting for the show to begin. I still have a picture of her modeling her purchases . . . of course the funny part was seeing her put on these 'little' items over her jeans and blouse.

I always told them when they visited me in the mountains that the economy of North Carolina improved because of our shopping trips. During our 'Show and Tell' when one girl would pull out an item, you could hear, "Oh I love that, where did you find that? We must go back to that store tomorrow!" There have been times when we were so successful in our shopping trips that the trunks of the two vehicles they drove up were completely full and I'd be responsible for bringing home the rest with me. I've hauled bedspreads, small pieces of furniture, and flowers in my SUV. I always wondered if this group ever shopped at home for anything. Of course, we never bought anything that wasn't *absolutely* useful or needed. Do we ever?

We have some wonderful gourmet cooks in our group and enjoy times they invite us for dinner in their homes. We just sit around the dining table and talk for hours, laughing, sometimes crying, but always coming away feeling that we have shared in the lives of our other 'Magnolia' sisters. Then we have some who do not like to cook. (I'm one of them). The little magnet on my refrigerator says it all: *'The only reason I have a kitchen is because it came with the house.'* Fortunately our group just loves to eat so a trip to Wings & Ale for chicken wings is always a real treat. Who would think that eight little 'ole ladies in their 70's now could put away a platter of 100 wings. It's true! The waiters just look at us in disbelief. Especially when we order the *HOT* wings.

This group is so blessed with numerous talents that compliment one another. There is no competition, or jealousy among the group. We have been together almost 20 years now and I cannot ever recall a serious, or hurtful dispute between any one of the eight girls. Oh yes, we do have different opinions, especially on politics, and we debate them, but we always respect one another's feelings and opinions. In the years we have been together as this special group of friends, we have not missed one month of getting together. Sometimes circumstances prevent everyone from getting together, but our unwritten policy regarding our outings, is that if we don't RSVP in the negative, we will be present.

'It is my joy in life to find
At every turning of the road,
The strong arm of a comrade kind
To help me onward with my load.
And since I have no gold to give,
And love alone must make amends
My only prayer is, while I live—
God make me worthy of my friends.'
—Frank Dempster Sherman—

One of the great qualities of our '*Magnolia*' group of friends is their passion to give and to help their fellowman. Each one of the eight is involved with their family, church, community and seeks ways to make a difference in others' lives. It makes me proud to call them *FRIENDS*.

If I had to tell someone what the happiest time of my life has been, it would be very difficult to identify just one event, or period of time. My life has been filled with so many events and situations, that I feel I have enjoyed a pretty well-rounded life. I believe that you cannot have a complete life unless, and until you have experienced every phase of life, which includes the happy, the sad, the sickness and the healthy, and the gratefulness for all that God has allowed you to go through in life

I believe the Bible when it says, 'There is a right time for everything'.

(Ecclesiastes 3: 1-8) (TLB)

A time to be born, a time to die;

A time to plant; a time to harvest,

A time to kill; a time to heal,

A time to destroy; a time to rebuild,

A time to cry; a time to laugh,

A time to grieve; a time to dance,

A time for scattering stones; a time for gathering stones,

A time to hug; a time not to hug,

A time to find; a time to lose,

A time for keeping; a time for throwing away,

A time to tear; a time to repair,

A time to be quiet; a time to speak up,

A time for loving; a time for hating,

A time for war; a time for peace.

We don't learn our greatest lessons in life from enjoying only the good times we have. The greatest lessons and strengths come from the hardships we experience. These are the greatest teachers of all because each brings out the best qualities in our character. They *build* our true character.

Life for me as a single again had caused me to get involved in some activities and organizations that I found very rewarding. Having been taught by my parents that you do not just "take from life, you give back." From an early age of six I had followed my Mother to the "old folks" homes. I would hand out song books and help serve refreshments. Oh how we have come such a long way in our ability to care for the aging of our generation. The nice facility where my Mother lived for the last ten years of her life was so comfortable and pleasant. I always counted my blessings that she could spend her last years among friends and enjoy the beautiful lawns and flowers that were planted around her facility. I could not help but remember the times as a child that Mother preached to me that you must always be willing to share your time, and love with others. It warmed my heart to visit her at her assisted living home on a Sunday afternoon. We'd walk down to one of the sitting rooms where they had a beautiful grand piano. I would begin playing hymns, of course. Mother would begin singing, and soon the residents would start coming in. Some on walkers, some in wheelchairs. As they came, they began to sing. We would have a wonderful afternoon singing all the old hymns. Their favorite song was, "Jesus Loves Me." I would not trade these *precious memories* for all the gold in the world.

One of the greatest joys, for me, was my involvement in my church. There did not seem to be a sufficient amount of time to take care of all the responsibilities I had accepted. You would think that being single, and having no children, you would have plenty of idle time on your hands . . . with me it was just the opposite. I had tried to be involved with activities during the week so that I could spend time in the mountains. I had also become involved with the First Baptist Church in Blowing Rock and participated in the community activities on the mountain.

Each time I would ponder eliminating some of my extra curricular activities, it became such a great burden for me to make a decision which ones I could eliminate, that I would just continue with my schedule . . . and it was getting pretty full.

CHAPTER 20

I T HAD NEVER been an option for me to consider marriage
again. Life had been good to me during my first marriage.
In my mind it had been my *'forever'* marriage that continued
to bring back the precious memories we shared. That seemed
enough to sustain me throughout the rest of my life. There was
no question that Hubert and I had a love that kept us together
through his years of depression. At one point he had even suggested
that I divorce him so I would not be subjected to dealing with his
illness. That was never an option for me to consider, but I knew
he worried that I was seeing him at the weakest point of his life.

After being a widow for a number of years, there had been
occasions when I had accepted an evening out with a few
gentlemen. On several dates my mind would wander to the
thought, 'would I be willing to deal with this person the rest of
my life?' Always the answer had been a very clear and profound
NO. Not just *NO*, but *ABSOLUTELY NO*!!

My job had given me an opportunity to work with some pretty interesting men. I could relate to them much more than being around the female gender in the business world. Most of the women were married with children, and had many more responsibilities to deal with raising children, along with balancing a career. Some of them were caught in situations where they were carrying very heavy loads, without the support of a spouse. There were times when I wondered how they had *time* to be married.

One afternoon as I had rushed home to change clothes to volunteer for four hours that evening at our church gym recreation facility, I had a message from one of my neighbors who had lost his wife just a few months earlier. He asked if I would give him a call when I came home from work. Being rushed to get to my volunteer job at church, I did not respond to the phone message. As I was entering the church that afternoon, I met this gentleman coming out of the church. He asked if I had received his call and I said yes, but I was in a hurry and had not taken the time to return his call.

This gentleman was a great 'back-yard farmer' and was wanting to share some tomatoes with me. So when he found out that I would be home later in the evening, he asked if I'd call him so he could bring me some tomatoes. Well, without sounding ungrateful for his generous offer of tomatoes, I agreed. Especially since my diet during the summer was tomato sandwiches, or fresh salads with tomatoes. Now I didn't know this man very well. I was much more acquainted with his deceased wife through our community club. They were very good people, but I just had not known them well as neighbors. Even though they were members of my church, they were in a co-ed department rather than the single/widowed group.

After I arrived home that evening, I did give Bill a call. He came down with a basket of the most beautiful, and perfect tomatoes I'd ever seen. They could have been on the "Southern Living" magazine cover they were so perfect. We began talking and I sensed that he had become very lonely after losing his wife of 54 years of marriage. He had four children, all married, eight grandchildren, and one great granddaughter who was three years old. It took a long time to get familiar with all the history surrounding his children . . . and for someone who did not have children, this was not the most interesting conversation I could have had. After all, I had worked eight hours in my job, spent four hours volunteering at our church Christian Fellowship Center dealing with sports enthusiasts, plus small children running around the gym all evening. The clock was ticking into the late evening and I had not eaten anything since lunch that day. After we discussed all the family, the conversation moved to traveling. He and his wife had traveled all over the states and in Europe. The conversation became more interesting because we found that we had visited some of the same places and could share our experiences. We began to laugh as we talked about our spouses and our many adventures with our travels. Now the clock was hitting the midnight hour and I still had to take a bath and get prepared for the following days work. Finally, it became apparent that I was going to have to end this conversation. It had begun with a simple gesture of a friendly neighbor sharing some of his bountiful crop of home-grown tomatoes. We finally said goodnight and went our separate ways . . . I thought!

On Friday afternoon as I entered the house from work, the phone was ringing. When I answered, the voice on the other end was asking if I needed anymore tomatoes. Now how many tomato sandwiches can you eat in less than one 48 hour period? My neighbor, and now friend, asked if he could come down and visit . . . AGAIN! This was a situation that put me in a position of sounding ungrateful if I said NO, but it also could put me in a position of establishing a continuing relationship, which I was in no way interested in. But, since it was a Friday afternoon and I did not have to go to work the next day, I did agree that he could come down for a few minutes. It was a nice afternoon so we sat out on the patio and began sharing our daily routines with one another.

Bill had been retired for quite a few years, and of course I was still working. We established the fact right away that he was sixteen years my senior. For some reason this gave me a sense of security. It felt like we were just two neighbors sharing memories. It was obvious that Bill had already begun to feel the loneliness of losing his wife. I was trying to convince him that, in time, he would probably meet some nice lady who would be interested in sharing dinner with him. Using my years of experience of being alone and having to adjust to a new lifestyle after my husband died, it seemed the right advice, and best consolation I could offer. Life would go on. You grieve, you hold on to your precious memories, and you make the necessary adjustments. You accept your situation at the moment and live each day that God allows you to breath. You focus on your family, home and friends and try to fill every waking hour with activities that will "make you happy." And of course, . . . you pray for God's strength and direction each day.

As we talked, we both found that we had many things in common. We both liked to travel. We loved to garden. We both loved to eat, and we had the common thread of being Christians. Now this conversation was on Friday afternoon . . . two days after we had initially exchanged tomatoes and the lengthy conversation that lasted until after midnight on Wednesday. You'd think there would not be so much to talk about. It was almost like we had both been locked in a closet for years without any conversation with the outside world. We talked about every subject imaginable and found ourselves laughing about so many experiences we both had encountered.

The afternoon had quickly turned into the late evening. That night I began bringing up the ladies of the church, and community that would be delighted to, not only share his wonderful tomatoes, but would be honored to have him escort them to dinner or a movie. It is a fact that it is much more difficult for most men to live alone after losing their spouse, no matter the years they were happily married. Generally, women make the adjustment of their loss quicker because of the many responsibilities of taking care of a home and family. Women also tend to involve themselves in activities, such as church or community groups. Their tendency to share their feelings is helpful in dealing with the loss of a spouse. Allowing a friend or relative to talk about the person whom they have lost is the best medicine you could give them. Good listeners are hard to find, especially about a sad subject like death.

I was always used to coming home from work, changing clothes and getting out in my yard for a few hours taking care of the lawn before the weekend. I would come in after my yard work and fix a little dinner, which I would usually eat on a TV tray catching up on the news of the day. I'd read for a while, take a bath and go to bed. On Saturdays I always made a visit during the day to see my Mother at the assisted living facility where she lived. We would go out for lunch, or dinner, then we would spend the rest of our time sitting on the porch just chatting, like we used to do as mother/daughter. Mom was getting pretty confused at this point in her life and, although she could have the most delightful conversation with you, non-stop, some of the facts and stories were not exactly correct, at least not chronologically. That did not at all bother me, because Mother had the most optimistic disposition and outlook on life, she laughed at situations that had taken place at the facility, and there were many. She would always say, "Baby, I'm so glad you came to see me today, it's been such a long time since we talked" . . . and that could have been only the day before when I had visited her on many occasions.

Mom always cheered *me* up on my visits. Those visits are special memories.

All of my friends loved my Mother. They showed their affection by driving a 35 mile distance just to sit with her on the porches, or take her out for a cup of coffee and dessert. I grew up having 'tea-parties'. As I became a teenager, we would make our trips downtown to Main Street and have our little 'tea-party'. Sometimes we would park on Main Street, buy a bag of popcorn and a drink from the vendor who ran a little stand outside Silver's Dime Store where we liked to browse. We'd sit in the car and people watch. That too is one of my *precious memories.*

As we continued this tradition through the years, Mother and I found so many little places that we could share our coffee and dessert or sweet roll. In the small town where she made her home at the assisted living facility, there were few places to eat. On Sundays when I visited after church, we would sit on the porch and rock for a while, then I'd say, "mom, are you ready to go for our *tea party?*" She would begin to get her pocketbook and we would be off to McDonald's. She was always amazed that we could get two cups of coffee and two fried apple pies for $1.50. I guess you could say that my Mother and I could have a tea-party almost anywhere.

One of the famous restaurants in Batesburg where Mom lived was Shealy's. It was a family owned Bar-B-Que restaurant that people came from all over the state to eat so they could get a tray of *pulley-bones.* This part of the chicken is almost non-existent anymore the way restaurants cut up chicken. Shealy's also had any type vegetable you could think of, all of which were cooked with the Southern delicacy called FATBACK. As a result, you could always find a large tray of fried out fatback strips that were crispy and salty, another delicacy that people loved to eat. (Is there any wonder that most Southerners tend to be a bit 'over-weight'?) We *love* our *fried* foods.

At this time in my life, I felt that God was closing some doors for me; but as He did this, it seemed He was also opening a few windows.

Sometimes I feel so grateful that I cannot predict the future. I have not always felt this way. My nature has, for the most part, been to plan and prepare for my future. I still believe in following this plan. Looking back over my life up this point, I realized that God had prepared me for many of the experiences I had lived through. My early desire for a career had been to be a nurse. Although I never received a certificate for nursing, I did learn through times of care giving that you need to have a strong faith and compassion for people to best meet their needs. Both of my parents taught me, through their example, to have a strong faith in God and showed me how to be compassionate to the needs of others.

Now, the situation with my neighbor Bill had been developing into a more frequent 'consulting visitation'. On the Saturday morning after we had spent so much time discussing his lonely days and how he could begin to handle this, he called early to say he was bringing me another basket of tomatoes. I asked him what he thought I would do with a whole basket of tomatoes. He said, "well, you can always freeze them." Now I was not the little Betty Crocker, Martha Stewart domestic he thought I was because I had never frozen any type vegetable, and knew nothing about the process. I suggested several ladies in the church who would just love to have some home-grown tomatoes. This did not discourage him in the least. He wanted me to have this basket of tomatoes. So I told him to leave them on the patio and I would take care of them when I came home from visiting Mother. While I was having lunch with Mother, I asked her if she could tell me how to freeze tomatoes. She gave me some instructions. When I got home, sure enough, I found a big basket of the most picture perfect tomatoes sitting on my patio table. I didn't know whether to be happy and grateful for Bill's kindness and generosity, or to take them up to his house and tell him to freeze them himself.

It was the 15th of July and the heat index that day was 107 degrees. I went in, changed clothes and proceeded to find every big cooking pot in my kitchen. I washed the tomatoes, put them in the pots to cook them like Mom said. With all the burners going on the stove causing steam to rise from each pot, I was sweating buckets, the air conditioning and ceiling fans in the house were going full blast. I had slimy tomatoes all over the stove, cabinets and my beautiful new tiled floor. At this moment I could not think of one nice thing about Bill and his tomatoes.

Guess I was being very ungrateful but this just wasn't my most enjoyable moment. While I was in this state of mind, and mess, the phone rang and guess who? This very pleasant voice said, "hey Jo, did you find the tomatoes on your patio?" Now my first inclination was to say something that I would totally regret or be ashamed of later, like . . . "don't you even think of showing up at my house again with tomatoes." I could not be that ungrateful! He did offer to come down and help, but I graciously declined.

On Monday afternoon I volunteered again for the CFC at our church for another four hours. I went straight from work. I had not been at the desk very long until I looked up and there was Bill coming in the door. Since he was a member of the church, I assumed he had come to walk on the track or work out in the weight room. Neither of these assumptions was correct. He had come to 'keep me company'. Now the gym was filled with kids playing basketball, people walking or the track, the exercise and weight room was pretty full and the racket ball courts were occupied. The last thing I needed was "company."

Somehow I was beginning to feel that Bill was taking advantage of my free 'counseling' time. I needed to find a way to direct his attention to some of the other ladies in the church who were eager to make a new friend, and be the recipient of some nice tomatoes. As I was taught by my Mother to never hurt people's feelings, I had to give serious thought as to the most friendly, and diplomatic way to handle this situation. The opportunity opened up when he asked if he could come by for a cup of coffee after I finished my time at the CFC that night. This was going to be the perfect time to make my suggestion. I said yes.

At 10:00 that night I closed the CFC building and went home. Bill was sitting in my driveway waiting for me. Now it had been a very long time since I had eaten anything so after I got everything brought inside, I asked him if he'd like to have a 'tomato and egg sandwich'. He said he'd never had a 'tomato and egg sandwich'. I couldn't believe this. Anyone who grew tomatoes by the bushels must have eaten them fixed a million ways. I grew up eating 'tomato and egg' sandwiches. It was now 10:30 at night, I was in the kitchen making sandwiches. I guess it was considered a midnight snack at this hour. Anyway, this was the first "meal" he ever ate at my house. He loved it! Says to this day it was the best sandwich he ever tasted.

I had practiced all the way home how I was going to break it to Bill that, even though I had enjoyed our times sharing memories of various things, and appreciated his thoughtfulness in bringing me so many tomatoes, my life was filled with work, taking care of Mother, enjoying my mountain house with my friends, and being involved with church, community, volunteering at the hospital and keeping up the three houses now my responsibility. There didn't seem to be much leisure time, but I was happy and content.

While we were finishing our midnight snack, which was almost the truth now, Bill looked over at me and asked, "would you consider having dinner with me Friday night?" Without even thinking about it I said, "NO"! I then told him that I never had *me* in mind when I was suggesting that he could ask some of the ladies to dinner. I also told him that it was entirely too soon for him to be thinking about this. I was thinking long-term when I had suggested this idea to him. I asked him what his children would say if they thought he was asking a lady friend out for dinner this soon after their mother had died. He said he understood. He left my house around 12:15 a.m. I figured I had given him enough to think about and had been honest enough with him about my status that it would discourage him from calling or visiting me. And, that was my intention.

On Wednesday afternoon he called me to ask if he could drop by after he attended church. He just wanted to tell me one thing. I was finishing my dinner and watching TV, fully planning on making it an early-to-bed night when Bill arrived. He came in, sat down, looked me in the eye and said, "well, I thought about what you told me to do about going out with a lady friend. I called all of my children and told them that I had met this lovely lady who was a Christian, attended the same church, was widowed with no children and I was thinking about inviting her out for dinner." I asked them how they felt about it and they each said, "Dad, you go for it." "So, I'm here to invite you to have dinner with me on Friday night." Whoa now. . . . This little piece of counseling had really backfired on me. What was I going to do with this man?!

Again I explained that I was not interested in a relationship and saw no need to get involved any further. There was no way he was taking this NO as a final answer. I was at a loss as how to best handle this situation. My first inclination was to escort him to the door and say, 'don't come back, go get a life'. I was getting pretty desperate, but I knew in my heart that Bill was a fine man who had displayed all the characteristics of a Southern Gentleman. He was interesting, had a good sense of humor . . . traits that would make it easy for him to win over some nice lady. It just wasn't going to be me!

My second thought was, 'why not accept one invitation to dinner to satisfy him?' After all he had been very generous supplying me with tomatoes, even to filling my freezer with them. So, I said, "Bill, I will accept an invitation for dinner this one time, under one condition. We will not eat at any restaurant where we will be seen by anyone we know." He started laughing so hard. "Why do you not want to be seen with me?" Somehow I thought that if I wasn't seen with him, or any other man, that it could not be perceived that I was interested in anyone. It was decided that Bill would pick me up at 6:00 Friday evening for dinner at a location he would choose.

Bill left my house and I continued with my plan of getting ready for an early bedtime. I was actually feeling emotionally washed out with this situation with him. I could not ever remember being pursued by *any* male friend so relentlessly, even when I was in my late teens. My early-to-bed plan worked for me. I slept well and woke up rested for my work day. I worked late on Thursday, went to the beauty salon as usual and then home. It had been a pleasant day. Work went well and I was completely at peace.

Friday came and I was sitting in my office, thinking how nice it would be in the mountains. I almost left work early to drive up to NC when it dawned on me that I had made a commitment to Bill for dinner that evening. That meant that this weekend would be out for a trip to the mountains because most Saturdays I visited Mom. Suddenly my sense of peace left me. I realized that this dinner date was probably *not* going to be the highlight of my weekend.

I could not figure out why this was coming across as being such an obstacle in my life. I had never had a problem making decisions and moving on. Most of my decisions had worked out to be good ones. Some had not been so good. The ones that had not been so good, as I recall, were ones that I had definite unanswered questions about. This was most definitely one of those 'questionable' situations.

When I got home that afternoon, I had only a half-hour to shower, change clothes before my "dinner date." Bill had not told me where we were going for dinner, but I didn't see him as being one that would be taking me to any of our elite, specialty restaurants in town. So I dressed accordingly for the "date." At exactly 6:00 on the dot, the doorbell rang. I was ready except for fixing my hair. When I answered the door, there stood Bill, dressed casually, but very handsome looking, with one hand behind his back. What was he doing? If this guy had anymore tomatoes for me, the date was off. I had eaten so many tomato sandwiches and salads with tomatoes that it was a miracle that I was not covered in an allergic reaction to all the acid. Bill greeted me with a big smile and handed me a beautiful bouquet of mixed cut flowers. He said, "I didn't have a vase to put these in, but I know how much you love flowers."

After I had arranged the flowers in a vase, we left for dinner. I noticed that he was driving across town, down some secondary road that I was only slightly familiar with. We rode and rode . . . Finally my curiosity got the best of me and I asked, "Would you please give me a hint where you're taking me for dinner?" He laughed and said, "well, you said you didn't want to go any place where you could be seen with me, so we're going to a fish camp up around Fort Mill." "You're kidding me right?" "No, no, he said, it's probably a place you've never been, I hope you like seafood." I could not refrain from bursting out laughing. I said, "Bill, you know what, this may just prove to be a very interesting evening after all." It seemed we rode for two hours before we got to the restaurant. I was beginning to think that either he was lost or that I was being kidnapped and taken across State lines.

Finally, we came upon this pretty nice looking seafood camp that had little room for parking it was so crowded. At least it made me feel better that we would be in a large crowd and the chances of our running into anyone we knew from Columbia would be slim. I had forgotten how nice it was to have someone come around and open the car door for me. To pull my chair out for me in the restaurant. To hold my hand as he returned thanks for our food. WOW! What was going on with me? This man, no matter how much chivalry he was using was *not* going to work his way into my life. NO WAY!

Our dinner went great. Good Food. Didn't see one person I recognized. That was good. No one to have to explain what I was doing a 100 miles from Columbia having dinner at a fish camp with a Southern Gentleman who looked like he could appear on the cover of AARP as just receiving his AARP membership card.

On our ride home we talked about what we had been doing all week. Bill told me how he had been so excited over our 'dinner date' tonight. I thought, 'this guy really does need something in his life to concentrate on'. When we arrived home, he again, came around and opened the door for me. All in all, it had been a very pleasant and interesting evening, even for me. We had laughed, and for the most part, had not discussed unhappy things that had taken place in our lives. It was getting late so I did not invite him to come in. I needed to plan my day with Mom on Saturday. I also needed to figure out why I had enjoyed my time with Bill tonight.

At the time things were going along pretty well for me. Nothing had popped up as an emergency that needed my attention. And then, on Sunday night I received a call from my sister-in-law that my brother Robert was in the hospital in Florence, SC with a heart attack. They were preparing him for triple by-pass surgery the next morning. I did not give Mother this news at the time. There were times in situations when I felt it could be upsetting for her to hear such news. I made the decision to wait for the results. I could take her to see Robert after he had his surgery and was recovering. It had been such a traumatic loss for her when my younger brother David had died so young. As she had explained to me at the time. Losing a spouse is a terrible lose, but losing a child is the greatest loss a Mother can experience. Never having had children of my own, this was difficult to understand, but I did not want her to have to even think of losing another son.

My sister-in-law, Bettie called me on Monday night to say that Robert had come through the surgery just fine and was doing well. She had suggested that if I wanted to, I could wait until the weekend when he would be feeling more like visitors to bring Mom down. She would call each day and give me an update. Since there had been so many times that I had taken time off for emergencies and family illnesses and deaths, I felt comfortable with Bettie's suggestion that I could wait until Friday to go down to the hospital. I went up to visit Mom on Wednesday that week. I told her that I may want her to take a trip with me on Saturday so I planned to pick her up on Friday afternoon, she would spend the night with me and we would make our trip. She never asked where we were going. She just loved going *any* place.

With each trip we would take, her response was, 'this is so nice, I've never been here before." She had made several trips with me to our house in the mountains over the years. Each time she would enter the house, she would walk all over the house, up and down stairs, which scared me to death. I could imagine her losing her balance and ending up in the basement, or rolling down the steep back yard. She would come back in the house and ask, "whose house is this? It's beautiful, I've never been here before." Her memory had pretty much left her at this point. But wherever she went, she enjoyed herself and could not wait to get back to her little lady friends where she lived to tell them all about it. She could never remember where she had been, but she would always tell them she had a wonderful time. There were times when she tried to relate to her friends where she had been and I would be in awe when she began to tell her story. We sure did cover in a lot of territory over a two day trip. Some of the places I had never heard of. It's so amazing how our minds can take unpleasant conditions and translate them in to 'Beautiful Memories" All of them very *precious memories.*

Friday afternoon I picked Mother up. We stopped at Shealy's Bar-B-Que Restaurant in Batesburg, her favorite place for fried chicken. On the trip to my house, she did ask me where we were going the next day. I then told her that Robert had had surgery in Florence and we were going down the next day to visit him. It wasn't necessary to tell her what the surgery was for unless she asked. She didn't.

It was a beautiful day to drive to Florence. Mom loved the outdoors and was so delighted to be taking a trip and seeing different things. We had been having conversations about many subjects and then I asked her; "Mom, what would you say if I decided to remarry?" There was no reply. And, I myself wondered where in the world this thought had come from. We must have driven in silence for another five or six minutes. I was thinking she must have been as stunned as I was at this question. Or she just didn't want to give me her honest opinion. That wasn't usually a problem for us to speak the truth to each other. When she did speak she said, "Well, I think that if you could find a good man who would be kind and good to you, it would be nice. You're too young to live the rest of your life by yourself. But, have you talked with Hubert about this?" I looked over at her, she was looking straight ahead and I realized at that point, that she still had not realized that Hubert, my husband, was gone. Now, there are some times when you don't know whether to laugh or cry when dealing with someone who has memory problems. In this case, I looked straight ahead and replied, "No mom, I hadn't thought about that." That was the end of that conversation. We just moved on to something else and the subject never came up again. I did tell Robert about our conversation when we got to the hospital. That was one time he had to hold his little teddy bear very close to keep from tearing his stitches open.

Mom was satisfied after seeing Robert, that he would be getting along nicely. She was ready to go home. And home for her now was Generations of Batesburg. It was getting late when

I finally got home and I had a message waiting from Bill. There had been many phone calls from Bill since we had gone for dinner. My schedule had been quite full now that I was planning on making the trip to Florence with Mother. I had seen Bill at church during that week and he was aware of the situation with Robert. He wanted me to call him when I got home. I was exhausted from the day with Mom so I took a shower, changed into my pajamas, fully intending to go-to bed early. It seemed that each time I made plans for early to bed evenings, something interfered. This time it was another phone call from Bill.

You know, I was beginning to wonder what I was going to do to discourage the phone calls from this guy. It had been quite a few years since I had been pursued so intently. It had also been a long time since I had been on anyone's schedule except mine. It wasn't working for me! I'm sure that I must have been a bit curt with Bill, because he said he knew I was tired and he would call me the next day. Before I had a chance to discourage that, he hung up.

The one thing I had learned about Bill, he was honest, he kept his word, because at 7:00a.m. the next morning, the phone rang. Even though I'm an early riser, this just wasn't the time of day that you called trying to "court" a lady. My plans for Saturday were to catch up on yard work, grocery shop, do laundry and clean house. On Sunday I had church until 11:00 and then went to have lunch with Mother. I felt pretty sure that I had my bases covered as far as not having any spare time to see

Bill. No Way! "Of course you have to eat some time", he said. Little did he know that I was *not* on a schedule of eating meals at 6:00am; 12:00 noon and 5:30pm. That schedule for meals had been changed the moment I left home years ago. I ate when I got hungry, and that was not very often. I could have a can of Vienna Sausages with saltines or a frozen chicken pot pie and call that dinner on occasions.

The next question Bill had was, "can I sit with you in church on Sunday?" "Oh NO", I almost yelled. I always sat on the right side of the church towards the front. He sat with his son and his family on the opposite side towards the back of the sanctuary. I sat with my 'Magnolias' and other single friends. Had sat in that pew since the new sanctuary was built in 1965. There wasn't room on 'my pew' for him. And, there was no way that I was going to get the gossip line going about Jo Ann courting Bill. Whew! That settled that problem for the weekend.

This story was getting involved. I felt like I was being 'closed in' on and something had to change very quickly. When I got home from lunch with Mom after church, Bill just showed up at my door. I had made the decision that it was time to be open and honest. That's exactly how he was feeling about our problem. He told me exactly how he felt about me, how he had prayed that God would give him a sign that I was the one that he was to ask out. I could not tell him that I had actually asked GOD to help me solve this problem, and give me that kind of direction. That would not have been honest. And at that point, I can truthfully admit, perhaps this was why I was having such a terrible time with Bill's intrusion into my life.

We agreed that we would both give thought to the matter, and agreed that we would seek God's guidance. We also agreed that we would not talk or see each other for several weeks until we felt we could work things out.

One week went by . . . no phone calls or visits. Two weeks went by . . . no phone calls or visits. And on Monday morning at 7:00a.m. of the third week, Bill called to ask if he could come down for coffee after I finished my volunteer job at our church. I said yes. That day at work, I seemed to have pictures in my mind of the sweet things he had done for me, the tomatoes, the flowers, dinner, the phone calls and visits. These had all seemed like nuisances at the time. I saw the kindness in his smiles when I accepted invites to lunch or dinner, and the conversations that had taken place into the midnight hours on numerous occasions. Somehow, either my mind or my heart changed. Was it possible that God was sending this man into my life to give me a love and joy that I had not experienced in over 6 years? Would He send someone who was 16 years my senior? Would He send someone who had quite a large family since I had no children of my own? Just how would this work out in my scheme of things I had planned for my life. I thought I was perfectly happy and contented. I did not need a man in my life to take care of me financially. I was pretty strong and self-sufficient, 100%

independent. That was the characteristic instilled in me by my Dad. Almost to a fault.

Everyone Needs Someone, whether they realize it or not. Had I come to this point in my life? What did I have to offer to someone whom I'd known for such a short period of time? My mind was reeling with questions. So, as always when I come to a turning point, I pray. My prayer went something like this:

"God, you have known me before I was born. You have protected me from my mother's womb. You have given me love and guidance from both parents. And, you have carried me through some very dark days in my life. Now I am confused and almost angry. I had a husband who loved me as much as I loved him for 31 years. He was my 'forever husband'. I have been alone for over 6 years, but never felt lonely. I love you Lord, I want to follow your will in my life. So, as you know my heart and situation with Bill, I ask that you show me the way to go. You closed the door on my first marriage, now please show me if you are opening a window?" PS: *"Lord, can you give me your answer before 10:00 tonight?"*

I left work, served my four hours at the CFC at church and went home. When I arrived home, Bill was sitting in his car in my driveway. Seeing his car, my heart began to beat a little faster. Could it be that God was actually answering my ASAP request?

I turned on the lights, Bill got out of his car, with his hand behind his back. When I met him at the door to come in, he presented me with the most beautiful bouquet of red roses I'd ever seen. He was smiling from ear to ear, and he reached down and gave me the most precious kiss I'd had since Hubert had died. There was no question . . . God had sent His answer . . . Bill had received his answer from God and the rest is history.

CHAPTER 21

Wedding Bells Ring on Valentine's Day

AFTER OUR BRIEF courtship period where we got to know each other, and each other's family, we agreed to get married. By this time I had lost my battle to remain single for the rest of my life. I had lost the battle with Bill that I was perfectly happy with my life. Bill had the approval of his children and we proceeded with wedding plans. Bill gave me a beautiful diamond engagement ring. We had eventually let our friends in on the 'secret courtship' we had been having and he was finally allowed to sit with me in church. On *my* side of the church, with *my* friends!

When I announced my engagement to *"The Magnolias"*, they immediately volunteered to help with the wedding. We had decided that we would get married in our church, Northside Baptist on February 14th, Valentine's Day which fell on a Saturday. We talked with our Pastor, Steve Cloud, about marrying us. Steve said he would council with us about this decision. Not wanting to show disrespect for my Pastor, I said, "Steve, I'm not going to go through any counseling. Bill was married for 54 years, I was married for 31. We each lost our spouses through death, I think we have most of the basics down as far as what it takes for a happy marriage." Pastor Steve just laughed and agreed that he would marry us.

The big day came. The church was decorated beautifully, with Magnolias, candelabras and red roses for Valentine's Day. My long-time friend Shirley Reames, played the organ and Ruth Pownall, my next door neighbor and friend for years, played the piano. We had invited our closest friends and family, and I only recall one couple who were not able to attend. Bill and I had decided to walk down the isle together and stand before the altar for the ceremony. Our former Pastor, Dr. Lonnie Shull sang '*I LOVE YOU TRULY*' which was a salutation Bill had always said to me each time we parted. Pastor Lonnie also sang '*THE LORD'S PRAYER*' at the end of the ceremony. It was a very beautiful, and meaningful ceremony, attended by our most precious loved ones. *"The Magnolias"* were invited to sit on the front rows as my special honored guests at the wedding ceremony. They had decorated the church, and the fellowship hall where we held our brunch reception following the wedding. The *Magnolia* theme was carried out in the reception hall as well, even the wedding cake had *Magnolias* on it. The first time I got to see it was when we entered from the sanctuary. My friends had taken over and made the place look like a "Southern Living Wedding."

For my Mother it was a very big day. My brother Robert had picked her up and brought her to my house where I helped her dress. She was beautiful in her light blue suit. Her hair was perfectly styled and, of course she had those nails manicured as always. Growing up I never recall a time when Mom's nails were not polished. Even when she spent a day working in the flower beds at her house without garden gloves. She could fish all day, fool with worms and minnows, but she always had perfect nails. She would never let me polish her toenails though. She said she didn't want to look like a 'floozy'. She was Amazing! My friends always said she was one of the most elegant ladies they had ever seen. She definitely had a polished appearance. Always dressed, even when she was fishing or working in her yard.

Well, Mom was excited when we were getting dressed for the wedding. Bill came to pick me up. Robert and some family were bringing Mom later. Never did I ever dream that she was not understanding exactly what she was getting dressed up for. She greeted various family members when they came to the house. She was always a very gracious hostess and loved to have people come to visit.

When Mother arrived at the church, she was escorted down the isle by one of Bill's sons who was an usher. She sat at the front with a beautiful corsage. She witnessed the whole ceremony. As Bill and I were going back down the isle after the ceremony, I had stopped, kissed her and presented her with a long-stem red rose. She smiled and winked.

When I said, "I Do," at the ceremony, I immediately became a step-mom to four children, eight grandchildren, and one great-grandchild. This was a wonderful 'inheritance' since I did not have children of my own. It made us very happy that all four of Bill's children participated in our wedding. It isn't often that you have the luxury of 'choosing' your family. I did, and they have been a real blessing to my life.

There were so many people at the reception, Bill was having himself a great time. Almost looked like a politician running for election. I had little time to spend with each family member or friend. Mom was sitting with my brother and some friends. She looked over at my brother Robert and said, "you know, this is so wonderful, getting together with old friends and family. We should do this more often." My brother looked at her and said, "Mom, you do know what this is don't you?" "No," she said, "*but it's a real nice affair.*"

After we got home from our honeymoon, Bill and I went up to visit with Mother on Sunday. We were sitting out on the porch talking. Suddenly she looked at me, pointing a finger at Bill and said, "Does he live with you?" There were so many funny times with Mother after Bill and I were married. She would come to spend the weekend with us. Bill would pick her up while I was home cooking. On the drive home she would look over at Bill and ask, "how is Hubert doing?" Bill would respond, "well, the last time I talked with him he was fine." No more questions were asked. She would come in the house, walk all around each room and say, "well Jo, I love your house, I've never been here before."

Even as Mother's mental condition had drastically changed, it was always amazing how she remained so happy and contented with her life. I think she was living in her own little world, and nothing could have taken away the love and appreciation she had for family, friends and nature itself. She would ride down the road, looking out the windows and remark about how beautiful the trees and flowers were. God in His grace gave her this special ability in the last ten years of her life. Mother suffered a stroke, two days after Mother's Day in 2003. She died two days later. It was exactly 10 years to the day she had entered the assisted living. She could find something good in every situation and in every person. The epitaph Robert and I had engraved on her marker at the gravesite was, ***"She was loved by everyone who knew her."*** Those simple words summed up her life on earth. Her desire was to serve God, her family and friends. And most everyone she ever met became a friend.

I always wondered why there weren't any occasions when Mom actually discussed Hubert's death. She had loved him as her own son. She was living at the lake when he died. She was a part of the Memorial Service for him. But she never discussed him after his death, other than when we were at the lake together and she would say, "I miss Hubert", he used to do this, or that. She remembered all the good times they had shared and how he looked after her after Dad died. He would go down to paint her house, build her ramps and put out special fish beds so she could sit on her dock and pier and fish. He took care of her boat and car. I always felt she had blocked the sadness related to Hubert's death from her mind. Or, it could have been the brain tumor that was found later had already affected part of her short-term memory.

Mom never learned to swim, but she would load up her fishing boat, go out into the big waters of Santee and stay until pitch dark. She did carry a life jacket in the boat, but she never would wear one . . . except when she was in the boat with Hubert. He refused to start the motor until she put on her life jacket.

After she died, there were so many of her friends, men mostly whom she loved to fish with, came to me with stories of how they would come upon her in her little boat out in the deep waters at almost dark. They would have to stop and make her pull in her fishing gear because she had "found a big crappie bed." So many of Hubert's friends would try to get her to tell them where she was fishing at times. No way. Those were top secrets. Only privileged people like Hubert would she share this information with. Mom would never fish on Sundays. At the time I thought it was because she felt it was a *sin* to fish on Sundays, the Sabbath Day. One day I asked her why she only fished Monday through Fridays. She laughed and said, "did you know there are people on this lake that would actually follow me to my fishing holes if they saw me fishing on Sundays?" It wasn't that she thought that fishing on Sundays was a *sin* . . . she just thought that fishing on Sundays would reveal her secret fishing holes or stumps. She was a 'clever little lady'.

We always celebrated Mom's birthdays with lunch or dinner at one of her favorite restaurants. Because the grandchildren were either working or attending school, it was usually Robert and Bettie, and Bill and I. The first birthday party after Bill and I were married was a lunch planned in Lexington. Because I was still working and Bill was working as a bailiff at Richland County Courthouse in Columbia, Robert and Bettie came from Manning, where they had retired to, and picked up Mom. Bill arrived at the restaurant with a dozen long-stem red roses, tied with a pretty bow, and presented them to Mother. She was thrilled. We ate lunch, opened her gifts and Bill and I took Mother back to her home in Batesburg. We walked in with all her gifts. She was carrying her bouquet of roses. The sitting room was filled with her lady friends who said, "Oh Miss Jessie, where did you get those beautiful flowers?" Mom just smiled and said, "from my boyfriend." She then tugged on my arm and whispered in my ear, "and what was his name?" Bill was right behind us and he just cracked up laughing. She never seemed to figure out what Bill's place was in my life until the day she died.

She would always tell me that, "Bill is such a nice gentleman, I just love him." Bill was so good to Mom. He was kind and caring. Always including her in events we had with family. After all, 'he was her boyfriend!'.

CHAPTER 22

Tragedy Comes, Again . . .

DURING THE SUMMER of 2001, I was spending time in the mountains. Bill was at home working and did not go with me. On Wednesday of that week, I received a phone call from Bill. He said that he had received a call that my nephew Adam had been killed in an accident in Florence. It was such and unbelievable shock. He was only 18 years old, had just finished high school. Bill didn't know any of the details. I told him that I would be leaving the next morning to come home. When I got to Columbia, word came that he had been traveling a back road in a blinding rainstorm on his way home from his girlfriend's house. He missed a curve and ran off the road. He had managed to walk back up to the highway to get help and was run over by an 18 wheel truck. He was killed instantly.

It is always sad to lose a loved one, but to lose Adam so young was a tragedy that was hard to resolve. The funeral was in

Florence. The church was packed with people. It was attended by his friends and schoolmates, some who spoke at his funeral service. My heart was broken, but it was harder for me to see Misty have to experience this loss in her life so young. She and Adam had a brother/sister relationship that was extremely close. They had been through some situations in their lives very early that made them cling to each other for love and support. Misty had been Adam's idol, and mentor. Everything he went to do, he wanted her approval first. Misty had been the stability Adam needed in his life. This tragedy happened when she was in her senior year at Francis Marion University. All I could think of was wrapping her in my arms and bringing her back to live with me in Columbia. This, of course, was not possible.

We don't talk about Adam very much. Misty has her special memories of him, and I know it is still difficult to bring him to mind. My memories of him are some of the most fun times Hubert and I ever experienced with Misty and Adam during their growing up years at our house.

While I sat at Adam's memorial service, I could not help but be grateful that Hubert did not live to experience this tragedy with Adam. With the depression he dealt with, I'm sure this lose would have affected him as much as losing a child of his own.

CHAPTER 23

So Many Sweet, (Funny) Memories of Mother . . .

THERE ARE ENOUGH "*MOM*" stories to fill a book. One story we remember so well, and still laugh about, was the day I took her to lunch at one of her favorite restaurants in Batesburg. Now Mom had always been a lover of vegetables. They were the staples at our house growing up. She was an excellent cook and provided well balanced meals for us. It was essential for us to eat our fresh vegetables. But, Mom had developed this habit with her eating since she had been at the assisted living home. If she had something on her plate that either she didn't like, or was not planning on eating, she would take her fork, push the items to the side of her plate in a pile, and sometimes take part of a roll and cover it up. That was that! She would not touch it again. She never made an issue or complained about anything. She just took care of what she wasn't going to eat.

I had gone through the buffet line that day at the restaurant and fixed her plate. She ate very little anymore, so I gave her a spoonful of green beans, some rice and gravy, one piece of chicken and a roll. As we started eating, I noticed that she began to make her little pile on the side of her plate with the green beans. (I never made a comment about it . . . I knew what she was doing). The restaurant had long tables in the dining room and people just sat wherever they wanted to, at any table they wanted to. We were having conversation and I noticed that almost every time I spoke to Mom she would ask me to repeat what I'd said. I simply asked her, "Mom, I've noticed that you seem to be having a problem with your hearing. What do you think is causing this?" She just kept on eating and finally, she said, "you know, I think it's the green beans." Well, the three gentlemen who were sitting across the table from us must have been listening to our conversation, because they almost lost their food when they burst out laughing. I just smiled at them and let it go. When I got home that afternoon I called Robert. I said, "Robert, I had lunch with Mom today and I think I know what's causing her to lose her hearing." He said, "Really?" I said, "yep, she said she thinks it's the green beans causing this." And, he said, very loudly, "WHAT?" I then proceeded to tell him what had happened at the restaurant. To this day, we always remind each other that we'd better not eat too many green beans, they may cause us to lose our hearing.

The one memory that will forever stay in my mind's eye about my Mother, is that she was the most beautiful lady I ever knew in my whole life. She was tall and slender and walked with such confidence and grace. She was always impeccably dressed and her hair and nails beautifully done. Although she didn't have many clothes, she had the ability to put them together to make many outfits. (I did not learn this talent from her). She loved her high heels, gloves and hats. She always carried a dainty little embroidered handkerchief in her purse. I recall as a little girl, if I became restless or fidgety in church, she would open her purse and pull out her handkerchief that had a sweet shrub bulb tied in the corner. It would keep me calm for the rest of the service. It would probably be difficult to find the soft, dainty handkerchiefs now in a department store. I bought one years ago in an antique store, brought it home and washed it. I don't have a sweet shrub in my yard, but I took a cotton ball, sprayed it with my favorite cologne and put it in my lingerie drawer. Each time I look at it, the precious memory of Mother is there. Mother's beauty was not "skin deep." She was as beautiful on the inside as her physical appearance was on the outside. She was a real "*Southern Lady.*"

Some memories need only be recalled *after* the person is not around to hear them. One such story sticks with me so vividly, especially as I have just described my Mom as a "*Southern Lady.*" This one occurred while she was in the hospital for a few days.

Mom always had a high tolerance for pain. This caused us concern, especially after she moved to an assisted living facility. Sometimes undetected illnesses would go too long before being treated. Such was the case when I received a call one day from her care-giver at the home. She said Mother was running a very high fever and was disoriented. They were sending her by ambulance to a hospital in West Columbia.

When I got to her in the emergency room, they had already diagnosed her with a severe kidney infection and had an IV going. The doctor wanted to admit her for a few days for observation. Since Mom's hip and brain surgeries, it had been necessary for me to be with her on doctor's visits, and especially if she was hospitalized. Since her brain surgery she had practically lost her short-term memory and got confused easily. I would take her to the doctor for a problem she was having. The doctor would come in and say, "Hello Ms Jessie, how are you today?" She would smile big and reply, "I'm just fine doctor, and how are you today?" If she had made the trip alone, I'm sure the doctor would have wondered what the heck she was doing there.

I made arrangements to stay with her 24/7. That evening as dusk fell, Mother became very restless and agitated. Nothing was making her comfortable or satisfied. This was so unlike her, because no matter how sick she ever was, she was always pleasant and cooperative. She had eaten very little, the nurse gave her medications and we began to settle in for the night. Because of her agitation, the nurse had raised the rails on both sides of her bed. She didn't like that. She had her arm with the IV taped down to the bed, she didn't like that either. The antibiotic she was given was causing diarrhea so the nurse had put an adult diaper on her—She *really* wasn't happy about that.

As soon as daylight ended, I made my bed in the lounge chair for my night duty. I quickly dosed off when I heard the rails on the bed rattle. Except for a dim light in the room, it was dark. I could see that Mom had one leg over the top of the rail and was working to get the other one over. She still had the hospital gown on from the emergency room. It had two ties on it. One on the top of the right side, and one on the left side in the middle. Something else she wasn't happy about.

Not realizing that she had already taken her IV needle out of her arm, I just stayed quiet to see what she was going to do. She kept looking over at me in the chair. I just reached over and pushed the 'Call Nurse' button to get some help with her. I waited, and waited . . . AND WAITED for a nurse.

For the next few minutes, I witnessed one of the funniest sights I've ever seen. Mom was 5'6", a slim and agile lady for 82. She pulled herself over the rails, very carefully—continuing to keep her eyes on me. Her gown, which didn't come to her knees, or cover her bottom, was now falling off her shoulders. She kept pulling on it. Her diaper was now sliding off her hips and she was trying to pull it back up. All this time she was walking around her bed pulling the pillow cases off pillows, taking the sheets off the bed. She straightened the sheets like she was ironing them—all the while just fussing and muttering to herself. She finally decided to make-up her bed, tucking in the corners of the sheets, just like she had taught us kids to do. Each time she passed by me, she stopped to see if I was awake. I just played opossum—trying hard to control my laughter. By the time she got the bed made, she was so frustrated with her gown falling off her shoulders, and her diaper had fallen down below her knees. She just pulled the gown over her head and threw it in the corner, reached down and pulled off her diaper and put it in the trash can and was standing in the middle of the room, stark naked. I still kept my eyes closed. I knew there was nothing I could do until the nurse came, and I was hoping she would not open the door and walk out in the hall.

After what seemed like an hour, the nurse finally opened the door and turned the light on. Mother stood there looking at her like, 'Well, what are YOU looking at?' Actually this whole little show had only lasted about 15 minutes. She had accomplished quite a lot in a brief time for an 82 year old, *sick* lady.

Thankfully the nurse gave her a shot to calm her down. They cleaned her up from the blood that came from pulling out the IV. She got another gown, and this time it fit. They also put a pair of pull up panties on her. She got back in bed, closed her eyes and went to sleep. I *laughed* myself to sleep!

I had survived the hallucinations when she had her hip surgery, but this was the first experience I had ever seen of what the nurse described as '*the sundown syndrome*'.

To this day I can recall this scene and have a big laugh. Mainly because it was so totally out-of-character for her. She was such a modest person. To see her 'let it all hang out' was hilarious. Even in a serious situation, there was a moment of laughter.

CHAPTER 24

THE YEARS AFTER Bill and I married were happy times. We traveled extensively. He always had his bag packed and his hat in hand when you mentioned going on a trip. We enjoyed our mountain house. He has a serious breathing problem caused by working around insulation in the plumbing and steam fitting business years back in the 50's and 60's. The mountain house was at an elevation of 4,000 feet so he had difficulty adjusting to the altitude there. Of course, the mountains are hills everywhere you go, with exception of a few parks where we could take walks around the lakes. One of our favorite things was our picnics in the parks by a little stream, or we'd sit on a bench in Memorial Park on Main Street, eat our Kilwin's ice cream cone and 'people watch'.

For twelve years the mountain house provided some wonderful times for me. I enjoyed having friends and family visit. But the house was actually larger than our house in SC. It was three stories. I had spent both time and money landscaping the property from one road to the other, front, back and sides. That was when I was single, spent more time there—and was a lot younger. Also, when I began my extensive yard projects, there were teenage boys on the mountain who could help with the smaller projects, like carrying large stepping stones down a 45 degree slope. They helped me plant shrubs and build stone walkways throughout the yard. It was beautiful, but required a lot of maintenance to keep it that way. I learned quickly in the mountains, you don't landscape the same as in the low country of South Carolina. In the mountains, you use the natural trees, plants and wildflowers to build your yards around. This was what made the yard so beautiful. All the work had been done using the hardy materials God had already provided. The cooler weather and misty mornings helped keep the flowers healthy and beautiful.

In 2004, Bill and I had made the decision to downsize from the larger home where we lived in West Columbia. This was not an easy decision. Bill had two areas in our backyard where he had been growing his vegetables, especially those beautiful, 'seductive' tomatoes. I use the word '*seductive*' because they were what started the romance between Bill and I. We had enjoyed, not only eating the vegetables he grew, but we had such fun preparing, planting and harvesting the garden. After planting each spring, we would wait anxiously to see who spotted the first tomato, or cucumber or squash. The most fun to harvest were the potatoes. I could not wait until he let me dig the potatoes. We would usually harvest enough from two rows to eat, share with neighbors and still have some left for the fall and winter months. I used to tease Bill and tell him that I never wanted to be married to a farmer, but this type gardening was a long way from being a 'farmer's wife'.

We found a garden home close to the entrance to the Botanical Gardens at the Riverbanks Zoo. This was not far from where we lived. It was still close to our church, the courthouse where Bill was still working part time. The front yard was kept up by the homeowners association and the back yard was already irrigated and landscaped. It indeed was a "spit across" back yard, but provided me with enough soil to plant my flowers. The decision was made to sell our house and make this change.

Mother had died in 2003. We sold our house in March 2004 and moved to our new garden home on April first. It was traumatic for me. Bill hung his hat on the rack in the laundry room and declared, "I love it!" I placed the furniture in the house, what would fit, hung a few pictures, and made the house livable. The two-car garage was filled to the ceiling with unpacked boxes of *stuff*. I got the house in order and took off for the mountains. The year 2004 had proved to be a very stressful time in my life to this point, and it was only April. Since Mother's death in May of 2003, I had worked selling her house and closing her estate. We had sold our house and down-sized, and I was mentally drained. Mother's death had brought me more loneliness and loss than I ever expected. Although I had remarried, Mom had been my best friend in the world. Even with her loss of memory, we shared some of the best years of our lives. I felt I needed to head for the mountains where I had found my source of healing, both physically and mentally over the years since Hubert had died. There was something about being in the mountains that gave me the quietness and serenity I needed to re-attach myself to God and find my sense of direction.

When I got to the mountains, I immediately began working in the yard. In early April in the mountains, you don't plant annuals. This was a very expensive lesson I learned early. You can have snow flurries up until early June in Blowing Rock, NC.

The spring came, the summer began and I was getting calls from Bill, "When are you coming home?" He had come up to spend several weekends in the mountains, but he continued to work at the courthouse. I could not truthfully answer his question. I had begun to make my annual trips to Lowe's in Boone for my gardening needs. I had purchased four carloads of soil, fertilizer, and bedding plants to replace the dead pots on the porches and decks. I already had someone come to take care of removing the dead tree limbs and get the yard in workable condition for planting my flowers for the summer. Working in the yard has always been my form of therapy. You can dig holes and pull weeds all day, and at the end of the day, you cannot recall one thought that has crossed your mind, other than where to dig the next hole, or plant the next flower. My days would begin at 6:30 or 7:00 in the morning. With enough caffeine from a pot of coffee in me, I could work outside all day without thinking of eating or drinking. (Maybe this was why Bill didn't enjoy the mountains as much as I did.)

One of my very artistic neighbors had helped me design a little yard sign that hung from a post in my front yard beside the front driveway. It had a picture of Grandfather Mountain in the background. An angel was flying upwards. The sign read, "*Almost Heaven.*" That had been my feeling each time I was at my house there.

The days passed by quickly for me. I was enjoying the wonderful cool weather, friends had stopped by to welcome me back to the mountains, and I was beginning to relax and recuperate from all the changes that had taken place in our lives so far this year. *I was happy.*

The mountains are not usually affected by many hurricanes, but 2004 brought two major hurricanes up through the gulf and touched the Eastern corners of Tennessee and the Northwest corner of North Carolina. Hurricanes Frances and Ivan did massive damage to this part of the mountains. It was common for us to feel very strong winds coming directly off Grandfather Mountain where they had recorded wind speeds up to 200 mph. There were times when you felt you needed to have safety belts on the bed frames to hold you in the bed. These were whistling winds that made the trees seem like matchsticks. It was an experience I had to learn to deal with early in mountain living. Especially when I was there by myself.

The hurricanes came only about two weeks apart. That summer I spent the most part of my time in the basement, listening to a radio, waiting for the roof to blow off, or trees to fall through the house. We experienced every type weather possible with these two hurricanes. Wind, torrential rains, hail, thunder and lightening, and some tornadoes close by. There had been flooding in some areas that washed out parts of the Blue Ridge Parkway. Some small towns were almost isolated from roads being washed out. It was a scary summer.

There had been times when I had felt that I should consider selling my house. Mostly because it had become more of a worry for me than it was pleasure. I would go up in the spring and get everything cleaned up, flowers planted, and the yard looking picture perfect. I enjoyed having family and friends come to visit, but it seemed that I was spending more time working than enjoying my time there. The house was three stories, the yard a quarter of an acre, all landscaped that needed to be kept up. Bill was still working and I was torn between leaving him at home and spending so much time away. This was not how a family should be living. The times had passed when I had handy men who lived on the mountain and could help with some of the maintenance work. The kids who had originally helped me in the yard were in college or married and moved off the mountain. Things were changing and I was getting older. I did not have the energy I had when we built our house 13 years earlier.

One afternoon, after the storms had all passed and everything had been cleaned up, I sat on my front porch in the swing and began to evaluate where I was at this point in my life. It felt like I was coming to another fork in the road. What were the most important things in my life at the moment. Was I just overwhelmed by all the drastic changes that had taken place in my life over the past year? Was I being selfish to hang on to my house in the mountains, just so I could come to find my peace? Could I continue to physically keep up the house and yard, and not be worried when the storms came through that there could be damages to the house and no one to take care of it? The list of questions began to get pretty long. I did not have answers to these questions. Some were personal ones, others were based on the feelings of others and how it was effecting them. How it could affect my marriage if I chose to stay in the mountains as much as I liked to.

As I had always done in times where I found myself dealing with situations that I faced, and needed help making the right decision, I looked to Heaven and began talking to God:

"Lord, you know my heart. You know my desires, and you know where I am at this point in my life. Material things have never been my number one priority. Your blessings to me have been abundant. But, I need your help in finding answers to my questions and making the right decisions. You are good. You are faithful. And you are who I turn to for guidance. I pray that you will give me a sign in this

situation. I Love You Lord. I put my faith in you to help me make the right decision. In Jesus Name I Pray. Amen."

There was no PS or ASAP request in this prayer. I was willing to wait on my answer from God.

Several days later, I was walking around the mountain, visiting with my neighbors. It was a beautiful day. The birds were singing, the tree squirrels were up and down the trees, the rabbits were sitting beside the roads, munching on greenery. The fresh air smell of the mountains, with their cool mist and gentle breeze, made me think of my sign in front. It was indeed *"Almost Heaven."* That was one of the feelings I had being in the mountains. I felt like I was closer to God.

As I continued my walk, I had several of my neighbors say how beautiful my house and yard looked this year. I thought that was truly a compliment because we had just come through some pretty bad storms. There were limbs and debris all around the yard, but I did not have any structural damage to the house. When I finally ended my walk at my driveway, the sunset over Grandfather Mountain was beginning. The sunsets were spectacular in the evenings. I fixed myself a cup of coffee, went out on the deck and sat to watch the complete sunset. When the sun finally went behind the mountains, I felt a peace come over me that I knew was my answer from God.

When I prayed, I usually poured my heart out to God. He already knew my circumstances and my desires. I usually asked for a sign from Him that would lead me where I should go. God never audibly spoke to me. He gave me a sign in the form of an inner peace or comfort. This was how He was speaking to me now.

This sunset was the beginning of another crossroads in my life.

I had retired several years earlier. I had been able to spend more time in the mountains. God had blessed me with good health, a good job, and friends and family to share my house with. It had been my refuge in times of emotional troubles. But, it was also the time that I should be looking to future sunrises . . . and these sunrises should be coming up on me in our new home in West Columbia. I would be exchanging my time spent in this big yard in the mountains for the "*spit across yard*" in SC.

It was time for me to downsize my responsibilities and direct my time and energy to my husband, my family and friends, my church and community. I had been blessed with this mountain home that had served its purpose in my life. It was time for me to sell and move on.

That night when Bill called, I asked him, "What would you say if I told you that I was thinking about selling my house in the mountains?" He was silent for a few seconds. His reply was,

"Why? You love that house and the mountains." We talked for a long time. I tried to express my feelings and how I felt that it was the right time to sell. He only asked that I be sure that it was what I wanted. I hung up, took a shower and went to bed. It did not take me over five minutes to fall asleep. I knew what I was going to do the next day, as soon as the sun came up.

Actually I waited until around 7:30. I called Bob, a neighbor on the mountain who was one of the leading real estate brokers in Blowing Rock and had been successful with selling houses on Misty Mountain. Bob was about as surprised as Bill had been shocked the night before. He said, "Jo Ann, please think about this for a while. I'll be happy to sell your house, but you know you cannot replace your house or view anywhere else on the mountain." I knew this. But I also knew that property on our mountain was selling at premium prices. My house was not an architectural marvel, in fact, I had drawn the basic plan myself. But it had the advantage of being at a location that had gorgeous views from every location. It was on a private mountain that was a desirable location for buyers. It was in perfect condition with beautiful yards. There would probably never be a better time for me to sell.

I did as Bob had asked me to do. I thought for two days, constantly. Trying to make sure that this was God's answer leading me. I placed a call to Bob on the third day after talking with him originally. He agreed to come over that afternoon and talk with me. When he arrived, I was on the front porch. We sat outside and discussed a deal. It was the first week in September. It was already feeling like fall, the leaves were beginning to have color. My plan was that he could try to sell the house until I planned to go home in October. If it didn't sell, I would take it off the market until the next spring. This was agreeable. He then asked me to put a price on the house. Without even thinking, I gave him a price. I was planning on selling the house fully furnished, down to the towels, linens—everything as it was. I'm not sure where the price came from, but he looked at me with a half smile, like *really*, do you think you can get that for this house? Then he said, "is that what you want me to put it on the market for?" I agreed. We talked about how he would bring the For Sale sign on Friday morning. He would put it on the multiple listing and would plan an open house for the realtors the next week. I agreed.

Sure enough, Friday morning at 7:30 I heard him hammering the sign in the ground. I had not even mentioned selling to any of my neighbors. This whole thing had come about pretty quickly. I must admit, when he knocked on the door to let me know the For Sale sign was in the yard, it did bring a few tears to my eyes, because he had placed the '**For Sale**' sign right next to my "*Almost Heaven*" sign. I was going to walk away from some of the worst, and some of the best memories I had in my life by leaving this mountain. There had been friendships made, a relationship formed with the local church and merchants. Those relationships went deep with me. But, times change. This was going to be a BIG ONE for me!.

When Bob had put the sign out early that morning, I had not even dressed or had my breakfast. I went back inside, dressed and was making coffee when the phone rang. It was Bob. He said, "Jo Ann, I have a family who is interested in your house. Can you find some place to go for an hour?" No joking. It was now 8:30 in the morning. It had only been a little over an hour since he left my house. Of course I could find a place to go. I turned off my coffee pot, got into my car and went over to Boone for breakfast. I made another stop at the bookstore then went home. The people had been there. Bob left his card on the counter. About two hours later Bob called again. He wanted to know if I could find some place to go, again. He had another person interested in the house and was almost in my front yard with them. I thought this was going to be a circus if this was what I was going to have to contend with all the time. But, I left the house *again*. This time I went into Blowing Rock and shopped at the Shoppes on the Parkway and had lunch.

It was around 3:00 in the afternoon when Bob called the third time. This time he wanted to know if he could come over. At 3:30 he arrived. He told me that he had a buyer for the house. The first people who came to look at it, bought it. They were from Florida, had friends in Blowing Rock and had been looking for a house similar to mine and wanted one furnished, if possible.

They were ready to put a deposit until the final payment, and it was to be in cash. Bob said the buyers wanted to close on the house and move in within two weeks. That would have been fine since I was virtually just walking out and closing the door behind me, but Bob had talked me into providing the buyer with an 'exception list'. That was a list of personal, or any specific items that I wanted to remove from the house or yard. I had given him a list after walking through each room in the house. As I walked through the house, I could only vision our house in West Columbia and the unopened boxes still packed to the ceiling in our garage. It made the deal even more perfect because I had absolutely no room to put another item in our new house. Just the very personal items would be more than I could bring home in my one vehicle.

This sale of the house happened so quickly. Suddenly I realized that this was the sign from God that I had prayed for only a few days earlier. And He was sending His answer as an ASAP response. Now it was my responsibility to act accordingly.

I phoned Bill and gave him the news. I could hear the disbelief in his voice. I would call him with the final details when I signed a written contract of the sale. The one stipulation I made was that I would close on the house by October 31, 2004. That would give me time to arrange for Bill to drive up and help me move my things. This date was written into the contract. My house had sold, I was closing the door on one phase of my life, and beginning a new chapter.

CHAPTER 25

... And then came *Daisy May* ...

THE NEW CHAPTER in my life began in January 2005 with the purchase of a beautiful little eight week old Yorkshire Terrier named **Daisy May**. She is my 'later-in-life' child. The joy and pleasure she brings to Bill and I, is making memories for the rest of our lives.

2005 turned out to be one of the happiest years in this new chapter of my life. My great niece, Misty had graduated from Francis Marion University in Florence, and was now living in Atlanta, Georgia, working with State Farm Insurance Company. She had met a young man who was the tennis pro at the country club where her parents lived in Florence. He was an answer to my prayer for her. I had prayed that God would bring someone into her life that would become her "forever love." God sent George, a very handsome and charming young man. They compliment each other in every way. They became engaged, and married in April of 2006 in Myrtle Beach, SC. She was the most beautiful bride I have ever seen. The pride I felt as she walked down the aisle of the church that day brought tears to my eyes as I remembered all the special times we had shared together.

Shortly after they married, Misty entered the training program at State Farm for an Agent's position. She would travel back and forth for the weekends. One Friday afternoon as she was driving back to Florence, I received a phone call from her. She sounded like she was pretty 'down-in-the dumps'. She said, "Aunt Jo, I have just been offered and agency, and guess where it is." With the tone of her voice, I was thinking it was somewhere that neither she, nor I was going to be happy with. She then almost yelled into the phone, "it's going to be in Lexington, I'll be close to you again!" WOW, I could not believe this. Lexington was a small town about ten miles from my house. This would mean that my little girl was going to be near me again. We would get to spend time together. All I could say back to her was. "*Really?*"

During the next three months, Misty came to stay with me while she was going through the process of getting her agency set up in Lexington. Those three months were such fun. George was still living in Florence, trying to sell their home there, and make a decision of exactly what his role would be in all these changes in their lives.

Misty and George now live in Lexington. She has her State Farm Agency and George is the Tennis Pro at a country club in

Aiken, SC. Life is indeed very good for them, *and* for Aunt Jo. Shortly after Misty and George were married, they established an Endowment Scholarship Fund at Francis Marion University in Florence, South Carolina, ***In Memory of Adam Robert Doub.*** I think this is the highest tribute Misty could ever give as a Living Memorial for Adam.

Reading, and writing in my journals have always been two of my favorite hobbies. Writing in my journals was something I started when I was a young teenager. At the time, they were called *Diaries.* They came with a key so you could lock up your secrets. My journals, like my daily "Things To Do List", have followed me through the years from my teens to this day. Writing in my journals was, for me, an outlet for expressing my thoughts and feelings, my hopes and dreams. I get them out and read them sometime. It is amazing how my life has taken me down roads that were never part of my dreams as a youth. Each journal, each path I have taken has shown me how flexible, how strong I have become in my life's journey. They have proved to me, that as I have put my faith and trust in a loving God, that He has kept every promise He made. He has used some of the happiness, and sadness in my life to grow my character. I like to think that I have become a more loving, caring, compassionate person today because of the parents I was born to. This was the *first* Blessing God granted me in this life. They taught me how important it was to put my faith in Jesus Christ, and trust Him with every part of my life.

This book, "***My Forever Memories, are Precious.***" was written at the encouragement of a dear friend. She and I would share our memories with each other through the years. She knew my family well, and we would talk about my Mom in her later years and just laugh. One day, she said to me, "Why don't you write a book?" Several years later I had a niece say to me, "Aunt Jo, why don't you make a journal of the things we talk about?" So, on a rainy day, I sat at my computer and began to write as memories came to me. Every situation or experience in this book has been expressed, as "***my very own memory***" . . . They are not necessarily written in any chronological order, but is was written, as I recall them, from the first memory I can claim as my '*very own*' at the age of five . . . and each day they become more ***precious*** to me.

There was a period in my life when I felt 'useless'. I had not achieved any earthly rewards or accolades for any specific thing I had done. I had the idea that I must have missed a *special calling for my life.* It had never been my desire to rise to lofty heights of success, but I felt like I was still searching for *something*. My goals had been rather simple, uncomplicated. To find love and happiness, like I had witnessed in my Mom and Dad, and the right person to share it with. That was my goal.

The road I have taken has not led me to fame or fortune. But, it has given me a life of peace and contentment. There are numerous people who have been my teachers, mentors and support throughout my entire life. There is so much each has taught me by the example they have lived before me. Their encouragement and love are priceless gifts to me. I treasure each person who has been mentioned by name in this book. There are numerous other people who have touched my life in ways they never knew.

"It is threads, hundreds of tiny threads which sew People together through the years."
—*Simone Signoret*—

My wealth is not measured by financial worth. It is measured by the love and prayers of relatives, friends and neighbors who have touched my life in immeasurable ways. The ones who were there to lift me when I fell, walked with me through the dark days, and help put me back on the right road when I missed some curves in the road.

When you come to a point in life, and can honestly say, "I have made "*friends*, not just **acquaintances**," you are indeed **a wealthy person**. And, . . . your years will be filled with '*Precious Memories, Forever*' . . .

AUTHOR BIOGRAPHY

JO ANN D. BROOME currently lives in West Columbia, South Carolina with her husband and six-year old Yorkie, Daisy May. She is retired after a forty-five year career in accounting. Other than writing in her personal journals since she was a teenager, and letters to the editor of her local newspaper, this is her first writing for publication. You may visit the author on her e-mail address: jabroome@sc.rr.com